CORNELIUS HARNETT

CORNELIUS HARNETT

AN ESSAY IN
NORTH CAROLINA HISTORY

BY

ROBERT D. W. CONNOR

 BOOKS FOR LIBRARIES PRESS
FREEPORT, NEW YORK

First Published 1909
Reprinted 1971

INTERNATIONAL STANDARD BOOK NUMBER:
0-8369-5647-8

LIBRARY OF CONGRESS CATALOG CARD NUMBER:
76-148876

PRINTED IN THE UNITED STATES OF AMERICA

TO
MY WIFE

CONTENTS

CORNELIUS HARNETT

I

SETTLEMENT OF THE CAPE FEAR

Cornelius Harnett was one of that group of
North Carolina statesmen whose leadership
during the decade and a half following the
passage of the Stamp Act, swung North Carolina into line with the great continental movement of the American colonies, overthrew the
royal authority in the province, organized the
provisional government, inaugurated the Revolution, led the way to independence, framed
the first state constitution, and set in motion
the wheels of government in the independent
State. From this group his conspicuous ability
as an organizer and administrator led his associates with entire unanimity to choose him as
the head of the Revolutionary government
where his great executive powers contributed
so largely to the success of the Revolution in
North Carolina.

Harnett first came into prominence in the
affairs of the province as the political leader of
the Cape Fear section,—a section in which
many of the best chapters of North Carolina
history have been written. Born the same

year in which that region was opened to settlers, and taken thither by his father when a babe of three years, Cornelius Harnett grew to manhood as the settlement developed from a wilderness into a civilized community. He entered upon his public career just as the palm of leadership in North Carolina affairs was on the point of passing from the Albemarle to the Cape Fear; and during the two decades in which he bore that palm, as its representative, the Cape Fear reached the highest point of influence which it has ever attained in the history of the State.

At that time the Cape Fear settlement was less than half a century old. Among the obstacles which had retarded its settlement, the following were the most important: the character of the coast at the mouth of the river; the pirates who sought refuge there in large numbers; the power of the Cape Fear Indians; and the closing of the Carolina land-office by the Lords Proprietors.

The character of the coast could not be changed, but those who were interested in the development of the Cape Fear section employed pen and tongue to change the reputation which its very name had forever fastened upon it. "It is by most traders in London believed that the coast of this country is very dangerous," wrote Governor Burrington, "but in reality [it is] not so." [1] The fact remains, however, that this

---

1 Colonial Records of North Carolina, III, 430.

sentence stands as a better testimonial to the governor's zeal than to his regard for the truth. A different spirit inspired a later son[1] of the Cape Fear who, with something of an honest pride in the sturdy ruggedness and picturesque bleakness of the famous point, wrote thus eloquently of it: "Looking then to the cape for the idea and reason of its name, we find that it is the southernmost point of Smith's Island, a naked, bleak elbow of sand, jutting far out into the ocean. Immediately in its front are the Frying Pan Shoals pushing out still farther twenty miles to sea. Together they stand for warning and for woe: and together they catch the long majestic roll of the Atlantic as it sweeps through a thousand miles of grandeur and power from the Arctic towards the Gulf. It is the playground of billows and tempests, the kingdom of silence and awe, disturbed by no sound save the seagull's shriek and the breakers' roar. Its whole aspect is suggestive not of repose and beauty, but of desolation and terror. Imagination can not adorn it. Romance can not hallow it. Local pride can not soften it. There it stands to-day, bleak and threatening and pitiless, as it stood three hundred years ago, when Grenville and White came near unto death upon its sands. And there it will stand, bleak and threatening and pitiless, until the earth and sea give up their dead. And as its nature, so its name, is now,

---

[1] George Davis.

always has been, and always will be the Cape of Fear.''

But the very dangers that repelled traders and adventurers engaged in peaceable and legitimate enterprises made the Cape Fear a favorite resort for others whose days were spent in plunder and rapine. Behind the bars that stretch across the mouth of the river scores of pirates rested secure from interference, while they leisurely repaired damages and kept a look-out for prey. The period from 1650 to the close of the first decade of the eighteenth century, John Fiske has aptly called ''the golden age of pirates.'' As late as 1717 it was estimated that as many as 1500 pirates had headquarters at New Providence and at Cape Fear. The next year New Providence was captured and the freebooters driven away. ''One of its immediate results, however'' as Fiske observes, ''was to turn the whole remnant of the scoundrels over to the North Carolina coast where they took their last stand.'' The names of ''Blackbeard'' and Bonnet soon became household words in eastern Carolina. The former made his headquarters at Bath, the latter at Cape Fear, and together they harried the coast from the Chesapeake to Florida. Finally through the exertions of Governor Spotswood of Virginia, ''Blackbeard'' was defeated, the pirate killed and his infamous crew executed; and through the exertions of Governor

Johnson of South Carolina, Captain William Rhett sailed to the Cape Fear, captured Bonnet and carried him to Charleston where the robber was hanged at "the tail of ae tow." These were decisive blows to piracy along the North Carolina coast and after a few more years the black flags of the buccaneers disappeared from our seas. [1]

The Indians of the Cape Fear "were reckoned the most barbarous of any in the colony." During the Indian wars of 1711–1713 they joined the Tuscaroras in a desperate stand against European civilization, and the province was compelled to appeal to South Carolina and Virginia for aid. Though the former generously furnished assistance, it required three years of the combined efforts of the two colonies to crush the power of the Tuscaroras and drive them from the province. Two years later the Yemassee Indians of South Carolina allied all the tribes from Cape Fear to Florida in hostilities against the whites, and North Carolina in her turn was compelled to send aid to her southern sister. Governor Eden sent Colonel Maurice Moore with the North Carolina militia to the Cape Fear where he struck the blow that finally destroyed the power of the Indians in that region. [2]

But the struggles of the Carolina settlers with the forces of nature, the freebooters of the sea, and the savages of the wilderness, to recover this

[1] Fiske: Old Virginia and Her Neighbours, II, 364—369.

[2] Ashe: History of North Carolina, I. Chapter XV.

splendid region for civilization, were to avail
nothing if they were to yield obedience to the
orders of the Lords Proprietors. The Lords
Proprietors resolved that no more grants should
be issued in North Carolina, but such sales of
land only as were made at their office in London
were to be good.[1] But there were men in North
Carolina who were not content that a few wealthy
landowners beyond the sea should prevent
their clearing and settling this inviting region,
and about the year 1723 the ring of their axes
began to break the long silence of the Cape Fear.
They laid off their claims, cleared their fields,
and built their cabins without regard to the
formalities of law. When Governor Burrington
saw that they were determined to take up lands
without either acquiring titles or paying rents,
he decided that the interests of the Lords Proprietors would be served by his giving the one
and receiving the other. At his suggestion,
therefore, the Assembly petitioned the governor
and Council that the land office in Carolina
might be reopened; and the governor and Council finding officially what they already knew
individually, that "sundry persons are already
seated on the vacant lands for which purchase
money has not been paid nor any rents," granted
the Assembly's prayer.[2]

Good titles thus assured, settlers were not want-

---

[1] Col. Rec., II, 238; IV, 296, 299, 300.
[2] Col. Rec., II, 528, 529; IV, 296.

ing. Burrington[1] himself, Maurice Moore and
his brother Roger, led the way, followed by the
Moseleys, the Howes, the Porters, the Lillingtons,
the Ashes, the Harnetts, and others whose names
are closely identified with the history of North
Carolina. Here on the Cape Fear they were
joined by numerous other families from the
Albemarle, from South Carolina, from Barbadoes
and other islands of the West Indies, from New
England, Pennsylvania, Maryland, and from
Europe. The population increased rapidly, and
by the close of the first decade there was a
number of fine estates scattered up and down the
banks of the Cape Fear and its tributaries. [2]
Large tracts of forest lands had been converted
into beautiful meadows and cultivated planta-
tions; comfortable, if not elegant farm houses
dotted the river banks; and two towns had
sprung into existence. The forest offered tribute
to the lumberman and the turpentine distiller;
a number of sawmills had been erected, and
many of the planters were engaged in the production of naval stores. A brisk trade had been
established with the mother country and the
other colonies. When the settlement was less
than ten years old, Governor Johnston declared
that the inhabitants were "a sober and industrious
set of people," that they had made "an amazing
progress in their improvement," and that the

---

[1] Col. Rec., III, 138, 436.
[2] Collections of the Georgia Historical Society, II, 52 et seq.

Cape Fear had become the "place of the greatest trade in the whole province." [1]

The first town on the Cape Fear was laid off in 1725, by Maurice Moore, on the west bank of the river about fourteen miles above the mouth. Maurice Moore gave a site of three hundred acres, while his brother Roger Moore "to make the said town more regular," added another parcel of land. To encourage the growth of the town, Maurice Moore donated sites for a church and graveyard, a court-house, a market-house, and other public buildings, and a commons "for the use of the inhabitants of the town." [2] The town was laid off into building lots of one-half acre each to be sold only to those who would agree to erect on them good, substantial houses. Moore then made a bid for royal favor for his little town by naming it Brunswick in honor of the reigning family. But the career of Brunswick did not commend it to the favor of crowned heads or their representatives. It never became more than a frontier village, and in the course of a few years, during which it played an important part in the history of the province, it yielded with no good grace to a younger and more vigorous rival sixteen miles farther up the river.

This second Cape Fear town was laid off just below the confluence of the two branches of Cape Fear River. It consisted originally of

---

[1] Col. Rec., IV, 6.
[2] Col. Rec., III, 261; State Records, XXIII, 239—243.

two cross streets called Front and Market, names
which they still bear, while the town itself for
lack of a better name was called Newtown.
From the first, Brunswick regarded Newtown
as an upstart to be suppressed rather than encouraged. Rivalry originating in commercial
competition was soon intensified by a struggle
for political supremacy. The chief factor in
this struggle was Gabriel Johnston, a hard-
headed Scotchman who, in 1734, succeeded
George Burrington as governor. The new governor became one of the most ardent champions
of Newtown and used not only his personal
influence but also his official authority to make it
the social, commercial and political center of
the rapidly growing province. Encouraged by
his favor, Newtown in March 1735, petitioned
the governor and Council for a charter, but the
prayer was refused because it required an act of
the Assembly to incorporate a town. To the
Assembly, therefore, Newtown appealed and
as a compliment to the governor asked for incor-
poration under the name of Wilmington, in honor
of Johnston's friend and patron, Spencer Comp-
ton, Earl of Wilmington, afterwards prime minister of England. The granting of this petition
meant death to all the hopes of Brunswick. By
it Brunswick would be compelled to surrender
to Wilmington the court-house and jail, the
county court, the offices of the county officials,

the office of the collector of the port, and the election of assemblymen, vestrymen and other public officials. Brunswick, therefore, stoutly opposed the pretentions of Wilmington and kept up a bitter struggle against them for four years. The end came in the Assembly of February of 1739. Apparently no contest was made in the lower house, for Brunswick evidently looked to the Council for victory. The Council was composed of eight members, four of whom were certainly of the Brunswick party. Accordingly when the Wilmington bill came before the Council four voted for, and four against it. Then to the consternation of the Brunswickers, the president declared that as president he had the right to break the tie which his vote as a member had made, and in face of violent opposition, cast his vote a second time for the bill. The Brunswick party entered vigorous protests, but they availed nothing with the governor, who, in the presence of both houses of the Assembly, gave his assent to the bill. [1]

Brunswick did not accept defeat gracefully, nor did Wilmington bear the honors of victory magnanimously. The feelings aroused by the long struggle and the manner in which it was finally brought to a close strained their commercial and political relations and embittered their social and religious intercourse. [2]   But Bruns-

---

[1] Col. Rec., IV, 43, 235, 448—453, 470 et seq.; XXIII, 133—135.
[2] Col. Rec., IV, 457—458, 607.

wick struggled in vain against the Wilmington tide. Nature had given to Wilmington a better and safer harbor, and this was an ally which Brunswick could not overcome. Besides far more important matters than the supremacy of one straggling village over another soon claimed their united consideration, and they found that factional quarrels and jealousies would result only in injury to both. After a short time, therefore, when the actors in the early struggle were all dead, when their animosities had been mellowed by time, and when danger from a common enemy threatened the welfare of both, their differences were buried and forgotten, and the two towns stood side by side in the struggle for independence. This union was never broken, for the ties formed during those days of peril proved stronger than ever their differences had been, and Brunswick abandoning the old site united fortunes with Wilmington.

Among the early settlers of Brunswick was Cornelius Harnett, Senior, of Chowan precinct. Bred a merchant in Dublin, Harnett left his native land in the early part of the eighteenth century and coming to the New World in search of fortune settled at Edenton, in North Carolina, some time prior to 1722. There he seems to have prospered. He married Mary Holt, daughter of Obadiah Holt, of a prominent colonial family, entered upon extensive tracts of land,

2

and soon accumulated an estate estimated in value at £7,000 sterling.[1] But his career on the Albemarle was suddenly brought to an unfortunate close. Allying himself with George Burrington, who had been removed from office, he became involved in Burrington's silly quarrel with Governor Everard upon whom they made an outrageous assault. The grand jury promptly returned indictments against both, but Burrington's influence was strong enough to prevent the humiliation of trial and conviction, and after several continuances a *nol. pros.* was entered in each case.[2] In the meantime, perhaps because of this incident, Harnett had left Chowan and moved to the Cape Fear, settling at Brunswick.[3]

At Brunswick he opened an inn, established a ferry over Cape Fear River, entered upon large tracts of land, erected sawmills, and became one of the leaders in the industrial development of the Cape Fear section. His political fortunes, too, seemed to flourish. In 1730, Burrington was appointed the first royal governor and upon his recommendation Harnett was appointed a member of the Council.[4] His career as councilor was brief and stormy. The Everard faction, who violently opposed Burrington's appointment, charged that in selecting his councilors,

1 Col. Rec., III, 332.
2 Col. Rec., II, 646, 650, 661, 671, 702, 705, 714, 717, 817, 819, 822, 831.
8 Col. Rec., II, 650.
4 Col. Rec., III, 65—86, 91.

his whole aim was "to get a set of persons that will go into any measure he shall propose."[1]

In this they were probably right, but both Burrington and Everard soon found that they were mistaken in their estimates of the men selected. In 1731, Burrington recommended Harnett for reappointment, but in less than six months they were quarreling furiously. Finding that Harnett would not go into any measure that he might propose, Burrington repudiated his friendship, charged him with base ingratitude, and in Harnett's own house denounced him as a "fool, blockhead, puppy, Ashe's tool, and this without any provocation or anything then said by Mr. Harnett."[2] To the Board of Trade Burrington wrote: "I am humbly of opinion Harnett's sitting in Council is a disgrace to it." His attacks had the desired effect, for Harnett, becoming tired of the controversy, resigned.

The closing years of his career were less stormy and perhaps more useful. During those years he served as a justice of the peace, as the first sheriff of New Hanover county, and as vestryman of St. Philip's Church at Brunswick. Dying in 1742, he left a not inconsiderable estate[3] to his son of the same name who was destined to play an eminent part in the history of North Carolina.

[1] Col. Rec., III, 123.

[2] Col. Rec., III, 365.

[3] MS. record in the court-house of New Hanover county, furnished by Messrs. A. M. Waddell and W. B. McKoy.

II

EARLY PUBLIC SERVICES

This second Cornelius Harnett was born in
Chowan county in 1723.[1] In June 1726 his
father purchased from Maurice Moore two
lots in the town of Brunswick on condition
that within eight months he should build on
them good, habitable houses. This condition was fulfilled, and thus the younger Harnett at the age of three years became a resi-
dent of the Cape Fear. He seems to have taken
advantage of such educational opportunities as
were offered him for we are told that "he could
boast a fine taste for letters and a genius for
music," and that he was a lover of books which
he "read with a critical eye and inquisitive
mind." He early became identified with the
interests of Wilmington and was one of the
leaders in the industrial development of that
town and its surrounding country. Growing
up with the Cape Fear settlement, he became
thoroughly imbued with the spirit of the new
country, of which the dominant note was then,
as now, high standards of personal integrity and
honor, and passionate devotion to that ideal of
individual liberty, which calls every man's house
his castle. The customs of the people, their

---

[1] State Rec., XI, 603; XIV, 254.

habits of thought, their feelings and sentiments, and their faults and virtues, all became his own. His intimate knowledge of their life and character, his sympathy with their ideals and ambitions, his wealth and his attractive social qualities, his genius and his culture, combined to make him the leader in the movements of which Wilmington was soon to become the center, and produced in him, as he has been called, "the representative man of the Cape Fear," and "the idol of the town of Wilmington."

"In itself," as Bishop Cheshire says, "Wilmington was an inconsiderable place until some time after the Revolution. But it was the center of a most cultivated, high-spirited and intelligent population, and, as it were, the stage upon which all the eminent men of the country around performed their parts. It was at once the head and the heart of the Cape Fear section. Its history is not the history of the dwellers within its corporate limits alone. The owner of a house and lot in the town could vote for its member of the Assembly, though he left his house vacant and lived in the country; and the qualification of its representative was not residence in the town, but the ownership of town property. So it came about that many of the most prominent characters in its history, those who were actors in its most stirring scenes, and who are identified with its memories and traditions, never resided within its limits. There were wealthy and intelligent and public-spirited townsmen, * * * but the greater number of its most eminent names are those of men living in the country around." [1]

Circumstances, as will be seen in the course of this narrative, made Wilmington the center of the movements which led up to the Revolution in North Carolina, and gave to its strongest men the place of leadership in the province. The town itself, as Bishop Cheshire says, "had no single man superior to Iredell or Johnston, of Edenton, but there were in Wilmington, and residing in the country around, a larger number of men than could be found in any other portion of the province of like commanding character and eminent ability." Among them were Hugh Waddell, John Ashe, Samuel Ashe, Alexander Lillington, Robert Howe, Maurice Moore, William Hooper, Timothy Bloodworth, Adam Boyd, Alexander Maclaine, James Moore, Moses John deRosset, and Cornelius Harnett, all of whom, performing their parts on the stage at Wilmington, wrote their names high in the annals of the Commonwealth.

Of Cornelius Harnett as a political leader, Archibald Maclaine Hooper says: "In his private transactions he was guided by a spirit of probity, honor and liberality: and in his political career he was animated by an ardent and enlightened and disinterested zeal for liberty,

---

[1] Historic Towns of the Southern States : "Wilmington," 235.

in whose cause he exposed his life and endangered
his fortune. He had no tinge of the visionary
in the complexion of his politics. 'He read the
volume of human nature and understood it.'
He studied closely that complicated machine,
man, and managed it to the greatest advantage
for the cause of liberty, and for the good of his
country. That he sometimes adopted artifice,
when it was necessary for the attainment of his
purpose, may be admitted with little imputation
on his morals and without disparagement to his
understanding. His general course of action
in public life was marked by boldness and decision.''

His public career extended over a period of
thirty years. In April 1750 he entered upon the
duties of his first office. In April 1781 he died. Between those two dates he was continuously in the
service of his town, his county, his province, and
his country. On April 7, 1750, Governor Gabriel
Johnston appointed Harnett a justice of the
peace in New Hanover county. In August of
the same year he was chosen a commissioner of
the town of Wilmington, and between that date
and 1771 he served in that capacity eleven years.
He entered upon a larger field of service in 1754
when he became a member of the General Assembly as the representative of the borough of
Wilmington. Twelve other assemblies were
chosen in North Carolina under the authority

of the British Crown in all of which Harnett sat for Wilmington. His legislative career covered a period of twenty seven years, embracing service in the Colonial Assembly, in the Provincial Congress, and in the Continental Congress. There was nothing dramatic about his career. He had no power, such as Hooper had, to stir men's passions with an outburst of eloquence, nor had he, like Caswell, the genius to inflame their imaginations by a brilliant military feat. Yet a careful and scholarly student, after a painstaking study of the records a century and a quarter after Harnett's death, unhesitatingly declared as his sober judgment: ''To one who studies impartially the annals of this State during the last half of the eighteenth century, the conviction will become irresistible that the mightiest single force in North Carolina history during the whole of the Revolutionary period was Cornelius Harnett, of New Hanover county.''[1]

Harnett's career in the General Assembly falls historically into two distinct periods. The first covered the years between 1754 and 1765; the second the decade from 1765 to 1775. One embraced the administration of Governor Dobbs and the French and Indian war, and closed with the coming of Governor Tryon and the Stamp Act; the other was ushered in by the Stamp

---

[1] C. Alphonso Smith: "Our Debt to Cornelius Harnett," in North Carolina University Magazine, May 1907, 379.

Act and witnessed the gathering of the storm which broke into Revolution in 1775.

Harnett took his seat in the Assembly in February, 1754, at a special session called to consider Virginia's appeal for aid in driving the French from English territory.[1] Throughout the struggle that followed, he took an active part in devising measures for the support of the war. Committees on which he served drafted bills for raising troops, erecting fortifications, and appropriating funds for war purposes.[2] Altogether the Assembly appropriated for the war more than £50,000. These appropriations, as the Assembly declared and the governor acknowledged, were all voted with "alacrity," though they imposed upon the province a debt of "above forty shillings each taxable," which was more than the currency in circulation.[3] In spite of this fact, the Assembly could not satisfy the demands of the governor. More zealous than judicious he allowed himself to become involved in a foolish quarrel over a matter which he was pleased to regard as an encroachment on the prerogative of the king; and rather than yield a little where resistance could do no good, he foolishly threw away the supplies which a burdened people reluctantly offered. Quarrel followed quarrel; the sessions were consumed

---

[1] Col. Rec., V, 192.

[2] Col. Rec., V, 193, 246, 693, 716, 846—848, 1084—85; VI, 136—7, 164—5, 319—324, 689—90.

[3] Col. Rec., V, 1001.

with quarrels. The Assembly refused to frame supply bills at the governor's dictation, and in an outburst of wrath he wrote to the Board of Trade that the members were "as obstinate as mules," and appealed for greater authority declaring that "there must be an end of their [the Assembly's] dependency on Britain if governors are not supported when they do their duty."[1]

But the real work of the Assembly during the first decade of Harnett's services was a conscious effort to readjust the relations existing between the Crown and the province. The efforts of the former, expressed through the governor, were directed toward strengthening and extending the king's prerogative. But the province having outgrown the weakness of infancy was beginning to enjoy the vigor of youth, and felt the paternalism of the Crown chiefly in its restraints. The royal prerogative had a way of interfering with measures which the Assembly deemed of importance to the welfare of the province, and men began to consider whether it were possible to get along without it. This feeling became so strong that Governor Dobbs, in 1760, declared that his authority ought to be enlarged so that he might "prevent the rising spirit of independency stealing into this colony."[2] Appropriation bills, too, occasioned some sharp encounters over

---

[1] Col. Rec., VI, 250.
[2] Col. Rec., VI, 251.

the constitutional right of the House of Commons to frame all supply bills. When the Council offered an amendment to the aid bill at the December session, 1754, drawn by a committee of which Harnett was a member, the Commons promptly rejected it, and unanimously resolved, "that the Council in taking upon them to make several material alterations to the said bill whereby the manner of raising as well as application of the aid thereby granted to his Majesty is directed in a different manner than by that said bill proposed, have acted contrary to custom and usage of Parliament and that the same tends to infringe the rights and liberties of the Assembly who have always enjoyed uninterrupted the privilege of framing and modeling all bills by virtue of which money has been levied on the subject for an aid for his Majesty."[1] Moreover a committee of the Assembly protested to the governor against the navigation acts both as burdensome to the trade of the province, and as levying taxes on the people against what they esteemed their inherited right and exclusive privilege of imposing their own taxes.[2] There was a long struggle, too, over the judicial system, the Assembly insisting on devising a system independent of the Crown, while the governor resented the efforts as encroachments on the king's prerogative. Cornelius Harnett served

1 Col. Rec., V, 287.
2 Col. Rec., VI, 1261.

on the committees which waged this fight,[1] but
they waged a losing battle for the king rejected
their bills and rebuked both the Assembly and
the governor for passing them. The question
of the number necessary to constitute a quorum
of the House of Commons also furnished a fruit-
ful topic for disagreement. The king instructed
the governor to consider fifteen members a
quorum, but the Assembly resolved "that they
would stand by their interpretation of their
charter and not enter upon any business without
a majority of the whole House."   An affair that
brought on a triangular fight in which the governor, the Council, and the Assembly all took
different grounds was the appointment of an
agent to represent the province in England.
The governor objected to any agent at all; the
Council insisted upon its right to a voice in
selecting him; while the Assembly was determined both to have an agent and to exercise the
power of appointing him without the interference
of the Council and in spite of the opposition
of the governor.

Aside from these political contests the work of
the Assembly consisted largely in planning
schemes for internal improvements. The population of the province was rapidly increasing,
its industries expanding, its commerce becoming
respectable, its social and political life, recovering

---

1 Col. Rec., V, 244, 693: VI, 140, 1154b.

from the turbulence of earlier days, had become
more settled, and the regulation of its internal
affairs demanded the attention of the Assembly.
Cornelius Harnett was an active leader in this
work. He served on committees to prepare
bills for the building of roads and the establishment of ferries; for the location of towns, where
no towns ever grew, and for the creation of counties; for the regulation of quit-rents and the
settlement of public accounts; for the encouragement of agriculture and the protection of infant
industries, most of which never outgrew their
infancy; for the organization of the militia
and the protection of the coast and the frontier;
for the regulation of commerce and the protection of traders; for the encouragement of
public schools and the advancement of religion
and the support of an "orthodox clergy." There
were few committees of importance on which
he did not serve, few debates in which he did not
participate. A history of his legislative career
for the years 1754 to 1765 would be a history
of the Assembly for that decade. [1]

---

[1] The proceedings of the Assembly during these years are printed
in the Colonial Records of North Carolina, V and VI.

III

THE STAMP ACT

The second decade of Harnett's legislative career began with the coming of Governor Tryon and the passage of the Stamp Act. Tryon took the oath of office April 3, 1765. At that time the Stamp Act was the chief topic of discussion in the political circles of America. The opposition to it in North Carolina brought to the front a new set of leaders and for the first time put them in touch with continental affairs. Among these leaders Cornelius Harnett was conspicuous. For obvious reasons, the Cape Fear became the chief scene of action in North Carolina and its course determined the course of the province. Tryon resided at Brunswick. He was a man of much greater force and ability than any of his predecessors. Courtly, versatile, tactful and resourceful, he knew how to win the favor of men and understood the secrets of leadership. If any man could have induced the people of North Carolina to accept the Stamp Act, Tryon was the man. But the men with whom he had to contend were men of equal ability and determination and had, moreover, far more at stake than he. Before his arrival they had already made up their minds what course they intended to pursue, and the Assembly, through a committee of which Cornelius Harnett was a member, had united with the other colonies in protesting against the proposed stamp duty.[1] When Tryon asked John Ashe, Speaker of the Assembly, what the attitude of the colony would be toward the Stamp Act, Ashe promptly replied with great confidence: "We will resist it to the death."

In this determination the representatives received loyal support from their constituents. Indeed, from the first, opposition to the Stamp Act in North Carolina was a popular movement, though directed and controlled by a few trusted leaders. In various parts of the province, during the summer, public demonstrations were made against it. At Wilmington large crowds gathered from the surrounding counties, drank "Liberty, Property and no Stamp Duty;" hanged Lord Bute in effigy; compelled the stamp master, William Houston, to resign his office; required Andrew Stewart, the printer, to issue the *Cape Fear Gazette* on unstampt paper; and organized themselves into an association by which they "mutually and solemnly plighted their faith and honor that they would at every risk whatsoever and whenever called upon unite, and truly and faithfully assist each other in preventing entirely the operation of the Stamp Act."[2] Tryon

[1] Col. Rec., VI, 1296.

[2] For the proceedings against the Stamp Act on the Cape Fear, see Col. Rec., VII, 123 et seq.

in great haste called into consultation a number
of the leading merchants, assured them if they
would not resist the Stamp Act, that he would
urge the ministry to exempt North Carolina
from its operation, and offered as a pledge of his
good faith to pay himself the duty on all instru-
ments whereon he was entitled to any fee. To
this shrewd proposition the merchants replied
that every view of the Stamp Act confirmed
them in their opinion that it was destructive
of those liberties which, as British subjects,
they had a right to enjoy in common with their
fellow subjects of Great Britain, and hence they
felt it their duty to resist it to the utmost of their
power.

The issues were thus joined. But no occasion
arose for putting the resolution of the people
to a test until November 28th, when the sloop,
Diligence, Captain Phipps, with a cargo of stamps,
cast anchor at Brunswick. Quickly spread
the news of her arrival. Up and down the Cape
Fear, and far into the country, men snatched
their rifles and hurried to Brunswick. Under
the command of Hugh Waddell and John Ashe,
they presented a resolute front to the king's man-
of-war, and declared their purpose to resist any
attempt to land the king's stamps. Captain
Phipps prudently declined to put their resolution to a test. A month passed, and Governor
Tryon wrote, "the stamps remain on board the

said ship;" and after still another month, he
added, "where they still remain." It is impossible now to realize fully just what such conduct
meant, but we may be sure that Ashe and Waddell, and the men who followed them, knew what
they dared when, with arms in their hands, they
thus defied the king's officers. Treason it was,
of course; but while the merchants and planters
of the Cape Fear might escape the penalties of
treason they well knew they could not, if the
situation remained long unchanged, escape the
penalties of ruin. Vessels rocked idly at their
anchorage and sails flapped lazily against their
masts, for Wilmington and Brunswick were
closed ports. Ships bound for the Cape Fear
passed by to other ports, and the merchants
expected nothing less than the total destruction
of their trade. Nevertheless, as Tryon wrote,
they were "as assiduous in obstructing the reception of the stamps as any of the inhabitants.
No business," he continued, "is transacted in the
courts of judicature * * * and all civil
government is now at a stand. The stagnation
of all public business and commerce, under the
low circumstances of the inhabitants, must be
attended with fatal consequences to this colony
if it subsists but for a few months longer."

With the opening of the New Year the struggle
reached its climax. Two vessels arrived at
Brunswick, the *Dobbs* from Philadelphia, and the

3

Patience from St. Christopher, neither of which had stamps on her clearance papers. Although each vessel presented to the collector a statement signed by the collectors at Philadelphia and at St. Christopher that no stamps were to be had at either place, nevertheless Captain Lobb, of the cruiser *Viper*, declared both vessels outlaws and seized them in the name of the king. Later a third vessel, the *Ruby*, shared a like fate. Captain Lobb delivered their papers to Collector William Dry that proceedings might be instituted against them in the admiralty court. Thereupon Dry consulted the attorney-general, submitting to him three queries: first, whether failure to obtain clearances on stampt paper justified the seizure; second, whether judgment ought to be given against the vessels "upon proof being made that it was impossible to obtain clearances" on stampt paper; third, whether the proceedings should be instituted in the admiralty court at Halifax, N. S., rather than at Cape Fear.

The passions of the people were profoundly stirred by these proceedings, but while the attorney-general was preparing his answer, they were admirably suppressed. When the answer was finally given, it was an affirmative to each of the collector's questions. Instantly the smothered flames flared into open conflagration. Wilmington peremptorily refused the usual pro-

visions to the king's vessels, the angry people
seized the boats sent ashore for supplies and
threw their crews into the common jail. Cornelius Harnett joined numerous others in a letter
to William Dry warning him against the course
advised by the attorney-general. A party of
unknown men entered the collector's house,
broke open his desk, and seized the ships' papers.
The people of the surrounding counties seized
their guns, hurried to Wilmington, organized
an armed association composed of "all the
principal gentlemen, freeholders and other inhabitants of several counties," took an oath to resist
the Stamp Act to the death, and marched to
Brunswick to rescue the outlawed vessels. It
was late in the afternoon of February 19th, when
they entered the little village before which lay
the king's cruiser and near which the king's
governor dwelt. Hearing at Brunswick that
Captain Lobb was concealing himself in the
governor's house, the "inhabitants in arms,"
as Tryon always called them, turned their steps
in that direction. Though fully determined
to seize Lobb and force him to surrender the
vessels, the leaders were equally determined to
protect the governor from insult. Accordingly,
Cornelius Harnett and George Moore waited on
him in advance of their followers and offered
him a guard. But they had misjudged their
man. Whatever else he may have been, William

Tryon was not a coward. He haughtily commanded that no guard be sent to give its protection where it was neither necessary nor desired, and with this rebuff, Moore and Harnett retired. Immediately a band of armed men surrounded the house and demanded the surrender of Captain Lobb. But Tryon stood firm, and peremptorily refused to communicate any information to the "inhabitants in arms," saying that as they had arms in their hands they might break open his locks, force his doors, and search his house if they chose to do so. But the leaders, having no quarrel with Tryon, were not ready for such violent measures; and learning in some other way that Captain Lobb was not there, they detailed a small guard to watch the governor's house and withdrew to Brunswick for the night.

The next morning a delegation from the "inhabitants in arms" went aboard the *Viper* and demanded the release of the *Ruby* and the *Patience*. The *Dobbs*, having given proper security, had already been released. Afraid to refuse and unwilling to comply, Lobb begged a respite till the afternoon. In the meantime he held a conference with the governor and other officials to whom he declared his purpose to release the *Ruby*, at the same time expressing his unalterable determination to hold fast to the *Patience*. Half a loaf to the people and half to the government, he thought ought to satisfy both. It did satisfy Tryon who expressed his approval of the division. At the same time he urged Lobb not to consider him, his family or his property as he was only "solicitous for the honor of the government and his Majesty's interest in the present exigency." With this understanding the conference was brought to a close. But the other party was not so easily satisfied. When the delegation from the "inhabitants in arms" returned to the *Viper* they dissented so vigorously, that Captain Lobb was forced to surrender to them both their half and the government's half also. He based his compliance on the ground that he did not think "it proper to detain the sloop *Ruby* any longer," and had suddenly discovered there were "perishable commodities on board the sloop *Patience*." But such transparent excuses could not deceive the governor. Tryon was utterly astonished when he learned that Lobb had surrendered completely to the people, and took him severely to task for his action. The detention of the *Patience*, he declared, was "a point that concerned the honor of the government," and Lobb's surrender of the vessel was a breach of faith for it made the governor's situation "very unpleasant, as most of the people by going up to Wilmington would remain satisfied and report through the province they had obtained every point they came to redress."

But Tryon himself was not to be exempt from similar treatment. It is true the people had obtained every point they came to redress, but their work was not finished until they had made sure no other points would arise that would require redressing. There could be no assurance of this, so long as there remained in the province any royal official with authority to sell stamps and seize vessels who was at liberty to exercise his authority. Accordingly the leaders made up their minds to take the same precaution against this as they had taken in the case of Houston. During the afternoon of February 20th, wrote Tryon, "Mr. Pennington, his Majesty's comptroller, came to let me know there had been a search after him, and as he guessed they wanted him to do some act that would be inconsistent with the duties of his office, he came to acquaint me with this enquiry and search." The governor offered the comptroller a bed for the night and the protection of his roof, both of which the frightened official gratefully accepted. Early the next morning the "inhabitants in arms" sent Colonel James Moore to demand that they be permitted to speak with Pennington. To this demand Tryon replied: "Mr. Pennington being employed by his Excellency on dispatches for his Majesty's service, any gentleman that has business with him may see him at the governor's house."

About ten o'clock Tryon observed "a body of men in arms from four to five hundred," moving toward his house. Three hundred yards away they drew up in line and sent a detachment of sixty men down the avenue to the door. The leader and spokesman of this detachment was Cornelius Harnett. Then followed the most dramatic scene of the struggle over the Stamp Act, a brief but intense interview between William Tryon, representative of the king's government, and Cornelius Harnett, representative of the people's will, for possession of one of the king's officers. Two better representatives of their respective causes could not have been found. Each was acute, determined and resourceful, and each sincere in believing his the better cause. Tryon, the ablest of the colonial governors and one of the most forceful Englishmen ever sent in an official capacity to America, "could accomplish more," we are told, "by the forcefulness of his personality and the awe inspired by his mere presence than other rulers could do by edicts and armies."[1] Cornelius Harnett, we are told, "could be wary and circumspect, or decided and daring as exigency dictated or emergency required." In the interview that followed Tryon had no forcefulness of personality or awe of presence which he could afford to hold in reserve; and Harnett

---

[1] Smith: U. N. C. Mag., May, 1907, 383.

was compelled to be both wary and decided,
both circumspect and daring.

Harnett opened the interview by demanding
that Pennington be permitted to accompany
him. Tryon replied that the comptroller had
come into his house seeking refuge, that he was
an officer of the Crown, and as such should
receive all the protection the governor's roof
and dignity of character could afford him.
Harnett insisted. "The people," he said, "are
determined to take him out of the house if he
is longer detained, an insult," he added quickly,
"which they wish to avoid offering to your
Excellency." "An insult," retorted Tryon,
"that will not tend to any consequences, since
they have already offered every insult in their
power, by investing my house and making me
in effect a prisoner before any grievance or oppression has been first represented to me." During
this conversation Pennington "grew very uneasy,"
and said "he would choose to go with the gentlemen," and the governor again repeated his
offer of protection. But Pennington was doubtful of the governor's power to make good his
offer, however good his intentions might be, and
he decided to go with Harnett. To the governor,
however, he declared that whatever oaths might
be imposed upon him, he would consider as acts
of compulsion and not of free will; adding that
he would rather resign his office than do any-

thing contrary to his duty. "If that is your determination," replied the disgusted governor, "you had better resign before you leave here." Harnett quickly interposed his objection to this course, but Tryon insisted and Pennington sided with him. Paper and ink were accordingly brought and the resignation was written and accepted. "Now, sir," said Tryon bitterly, "you may go"; and Harnett led the ex-comptroller out of the house to his followers who were waiting outside.

The detachment then rejoined the main body of the "inhabitants in arms," and the whole withdrew to the town. There they drew up in a large circle, placed the comptroller and the customs-house officials in the center, and administered to them all an oath "that they would not, directly or indirectly, by themselves, or by any other person employed under them, sign or execute in their several offices, any stampt papers, until the Stamp Act should be accepted by the province." The clerk of the court and other public officials, and all the lawyers, were sworn to the same effect; and as each took the pledge the cheers of the crowd bore the news to the enraged and baffled governor as he sat in his room keenly conscious of his defeat. The letter in which he described these events to his superiors in England, it has been truly said, "contained the most humiliating acknowledgment of baffled pride and irredeemable failure that Tryon was ever called upon to pen."[1] Their work finished, the "inhabitants in arms" dispersed quietly and quickly to their homes.

"It is well worthy of observation," as the *North Carolina Gazette* boasted, "that few instances can be produced of such a number of men being together so long and behaving so well; not the least noise or disturbance, nor any person seen disguised with liquor, during the whole of their stay in Brunswick; neither was any injury offered to any person, but the whole affair was conducted with decency and spirit, worthy the imitation of all the Sons of Liberty throughout the continent." This splendid record was due to the high character and lofty purposes of the men who led and who composed that body of men to whom Tryon always refers as "the inhabitants in arms." "The mayor and corporation of Wilmington," he wrote, "and most of the gentlemen and planters of the counties of Brunswick, New Hanover, Duplin, and Bladen, with some masters of vessels, composed this corps."

Throughout the contest Harnett and the other leaders received loyal support from the people. They were in the midst of it upon the day set by the governor's writ for the election of representatives to the Assembly. Wilmington manifested its approval of Harnett's course by electing him without opposition, and New Hanover

---

[1] Smith: U. N. C. Mag., May, 1907, 384.

unanimously elected John Ashe and James Moore. But the Assembly was not to meet any time soon. Tryon was too prudent a politician to convene a session while the people were in such a rebellious mood. He foresaw that Parliament would likely repeal the Stamp Act and hoped by announcing that fact when the Assembly met to insure the good humor of the House. It was not until November, therefore, that he ventured to face the people's representatives. He opened the session with a conciliatory message. But the members, irritated at his delay in calling them together, replied through a committee of which Harnett was a member, with such asperity and show of temper, that the Council denounced their message as "altogether indecent, without foundation and unmerited."[1] The reply cut the governor to the quick, but he kept his temper and met the strictures of the Assembly with admirable moderation and dignity.

Whatever one may think of Tryon, there can be but one just opinion of his bearing throughout these trying ordeals. He bore himself on every occasion with dignity, courage and fidelity to his trust. His dispatches even when acknowledging defeat are conspicuous for their good temper. We search in vain for the ill-tempered invectives and impassioned superlatives that characterized the dispatches both of Dobbs, his predecessor, and of Martin, his successor.

---

[1] Col. Rec., VII, 272.

Closing his letter to Secretary Conway, he says:
"Thus, sir, I have endeavored to lay before you
the first springs of this disturbance as well as
the particular conduct of the individual parties
concerned in it and I have done this as much as
I possibly could without prejudice or passion,
favor or affection." The impartial reader
will pronounce that in this endeavor he reached a
remarkable degree of success. Nor was his courage less marked than his dignity. When shielding
Lobb on the evening of February 19 and when
standing between Pennington and the "inhabitants in arms" on the morning of the 21st, one
feels sure that he would have seen his house go
down in ruins or up in smoke before he would
have yielded one inch to the besiegers. In this
courage straight from his heart originated his un-
feigned and unconcealed contempt for the conduct
of Captain Lobb. We feel assured that William
Tryon would have buried himself, his crew and his
opponents in the bottom of the Cape Fear river
beneath the wrecks of the *Viper*, the *Diligence*,
the *Dobbs*, the *Patience*, and the *Ruby*, all, before
he would have broken his engagement and
embarrassed his superior officer. His sympathies
were with the people in their struggle, and the
duty imposed upon him a disagreeable one, but
he faced it like a man and performed it faithfully.
The king had entrusted him with the execution
of the laws in North Carolina and that trust he

regarded, rightly or wrongly, as superior to any
obligations he owed to the people of the province.
He was not their governor; he was the king's
vicegerent, and his first duty was to obey the
commands of his master.

To say this of Tryon is not to depreciate the
honor and the glory that belong to his opponents.
To Harnett and Ashe and Moore and Waddell
and the men who followed them, North Carolinians owe their liberty, and no true American
anywhere will deny to them the credit that
belongs to those who see the right and fearlessly
pursue it.   Throughout the contest the "inhabitants in arms" carried every point at issue.
But the most remarkable feature of the struggle
was its absolute openness and orderliness.   No
attempt at concealment, no effort at disguise
betrayed a doubt in the minds of the leaders
that they were engaged in a righteous cause.
The resistance was made by men on terms of
familiarity with the governor, under the guns
of the king's ships, and in the broad open light
of day.   Conscious of the rectitude of their
purpose, the moral if not the legal right of their
conduct, they felt that any attempt at concealment would be an admission, at least, of a doubt
in their minds of the propriety of their course,
and this they scorned to make.

Throughout this contest the conduct of no
man stands out so conspicuously as that of

Cornelius Harnett. From the announcement of the British ministry's intention to levy a stamp duty in America, he was among the foremost in opposition; and it is stating nothing more than the records will bear out to say that when the struggle closed, no man could justly claim more credit for successfully preventing the operation of the Stamp Act in North Carolina than he. Circumstances it is true favored him. Wilmington was the chief port of entry in the province and Brunswick was the place of the governor's residence, consequently the Cape Fear became the scene of the struggle. When it began there were several strong, forceful men in the immediate vicinity of Wilmington and Brunswick capable of leading the opposition, but none of them stood so conspicuously above the others in leadership that he can be designated as the leader. The records of their earliest proceedings, therefore, are largely impersonal and it is difficult to say just what share each of the leaders had in them. Thus we are told what the mayor and aldermen did, what the attitude of the leading merchants was, what part the Sons of Liberty played, how the principal gentlemen and freeholders acted, but we can not attribute to any individual the credit for any particular work. Yet we know that Cornelius Harnett was the most prominent of the aldermen, that he was probably the chief

merchant of the Cape Fear, that he was at the
head of the Sons of Liberty, and that he was one
of the wealthiest of the gentlemen and freeholders
of the Cape Fear. What his share in the early
movements against the Stamp Act was, therefore, may be clearly inferred, and we observe
that as the struggle progressed the opposition
centers more and more around him, until at
its climax he and Tryon stand face to face, the
acknowledged leaders of their respective causes.
"Before this incident," as Dr. Smith says,[1]
"Harnett had been best known as a skillful
financier. * * * But after his defiance of
Tryon in 1766—an act performed ten years
before the Declaration of Independence and
seven years before the Boston Tea Party—Harnett became in an especial sense the leader of
his people and the target of British malevolence
and denunciation. Every State boasts its heroes
of the Stamp Act, but in all the examples of resistance to this oppressive act, I find no deed that
equals Harnett's in its blend of courage, dignity,
and orderliness. He and Tryon had looked each
other in the eyes, and the eyes of the Englishman
had quailed."

---

[1] U. N. C. Mag., May, 1907, 385—86.

IV

THE CONTINENTAL ASSOCIATION

From the struggle over the Stamp Act was born a union sentiment that contained the germs of nationality, and the development of this sentiment in the contests with the mother country from 1765 to 1775 gives to the events of that decade their chief significance. Cornelius Harnett enlisted heartily in this movement, and contributed largely to its success in North Carolina. So far, then, as North Carolina's adherence to the continental or national cause was a factor in its success, so far must we think of Harnett's work as of national significance, and of himself as entitled to rank as among American statesmen. How far this was will appear, it is hoped, as this narrative progresses.

The Declaratory Act, which accompanied the repeal of the Stamp Act, asserted the right of Parliament to legislate for the colonies "in all cases whatsoever." The Townshend Acts passed in June 1767, attempted to put this assertion into practice. Under a pretense of regulating commerce, Parliament levied duties on certain commodities, principally tea, imported into the colonies, and directed that the revenues derived therefrom be used to pay the salaries of colonial officials, thus rendering them inde-

pendent of the colonial assemblies. This scheme
gave a new impulse to the union sentiment.
Massachusetts led the way with the famous
circular letter of 1768 inviting the other colonies
to unite with her in protests to the king. But
unity of action on the part of the colonies was
the last thing the king and ministry desired, and
they saw in this letter nothing but an effort
"to promote unwarrantable combinations and
to excite and encourage an open opposition to
and denial of the authority of Parliament."
Accordingly they commanded the Assembly of
Massachusetts to rescind the letter and the
assemblies of the other colonies to treat it with
contempt on pains of "an immediate prorogation
or dissolution." But Massachusetts refused to
rescind, and the other colonies applauded her
spirit and imitated her action.

When the Assembly of North Carolina met,
Speaker John Harvey laid the Massachusetts
letter before the House.[1] The policy of united
action instantly found favor. Harvey was
authorized to return a suitable reply to Massachusetts, a committee was appointed to prepare
an address to the king, and the agent in London
was instructed to unite with the other colonial
agents in efforts to procure a favorable hearing
on the several petitions. The committee's
address to the king was an able state paper, and

---

[1] Col. Rec., VII, 928.

4

rang true to the American doctrine of "no taxation without representation." They reminded the king that their ancestors, when they settled in the New World, "brought with them inherent in their persons, and transmitted down to their posterity, all the rights and liberties" of his "natural born subjects within the parent State, and have ever since enjoyed as Britons the privilege of an exemption from any taxations but such as have been imposed on them by themselves or their representatives, and this privilege we esteem so invaluable that we are fully convinced no other can possibly exist without it. It is therefore with the utmost anxiety and concern we observe duties have lately been imposed upon us by Parliament for the sole and express purpose of raising a revenue. This is a taxation which we are fully persuaded the acknowledged principles of the British Constitution ought to protect us from. Free men can not be legally taxed but by themselves or their representatives, and that your Majesty's subjects within this province are represented in Parliament we can not allow, and are convinced that from our situation we never can be."[1] Along with this address went the instructions to their agent of whom they required "a spirited cooperation with the agents of our sister colonies and those who may be disposed to serve us in obtaining a repeal of the late act imposing internal taxes on Americans without

---

[1] Col. Rec., VII, 980.

their consent."[1] In the same spirit they declared
in their letter to the Massachusetts Assembly
that North Carolina was "ready firmly to unite
with her sister colonies in pursuing every constitutional measure for the repeal of the grievances
so justly complained of."[2] When this letter
was received in Boston it was triumphantly
declared: "The colonies no longer disconnected,
form one body; a common sensation possesses
the whole; the circulation is complete, and the
vital fluid returns from whence it was sent out."[3]

As a warning to the other colonies the ministry
selected Massachusetts for punishment. Persons
suspected of encouraging resistance to Parliament
were to be arrested and sent to England for trial;
town-meetings were to be suppressed; and two
regiments were ordered to Boston to overawe
that town. The blow was aimed at Massachusetts alone, but the other colonies promptly
rallied to her support and raised the cry that
Massachusetts was suffering in the common
cause. Virginia acted first. Her Assembly
denounced the government's action in a series
of spirited resolutions, and sent them to the
other assemblies "requesting their concurrence
therein." In consequence they suffered dissolution, but the burgesses promptly met as a
convention, agreed on a "Non-Importation Asso-

---

[1] Col. Rec., VII, 877.
[2] The Boston Evening Post, May 15, 1769.
[3] Ibid.

ciation," and circulated it throughout the colonies.

On November 2, 1769, John Harvey laid the Virginia resolutions before the North Carolina Assembly. The House, without a dissenting voice, adopted them almost *verbatim*, agreed on a second protest to the king, and instructed their agent, after presenting it to have it printed in the British papers. Convinced that the king was deaf to their prayers, they now began to appeal to their British brethren. They again denied the right of Parliament to levy taxes in America, affirmed the right of the colonies to unite in protests to the throne, and denounced as "highly derogatory to the rights of British subjects" the carrying of any American to England for trial, "as thereby the inestimable privilege of being tried by a jury from the vicinage, as well as the liberty of summoning and producing witnesses on such trial, will be taken away from the party accused." "We can not without horror," they declared, "think of the new, unusual, * * * unconstitutional and illegal mode recommended to your Majesty of seizing and carrying beyond sea the inhabitants of America suspected of any crime, [and] of trying such person in any other manner than by the ancient and long established course of proceedings." "Truly alarmed at the fatal tendency of these pernicious councils," [sic], they earnestly prayed his Majesty to interpose his protection against "such dangerous invasions" of their dearest privileges.[1] These proceedings, when reported to the governor, sealed the fate of that Assembly. Sending in haste for the House, he censured them for their action, declared that it "sapped the foundation of confidence and gratitude," and made it his "indispensable duty to put an end to this session."

This sudden turn of affairs caught the Assembly unprepared for dissolution. Much important business, especially the adoption of the "Non-Importation Association," remained unfinished. Everybody realized that the effectiveness of non-importation as a weapon for fighting the Townshend duties depended entirely upon the extent to which it was adopted, and the fidelity with which it was observed. Any one colony could easily defeat the whole scheme. When the North Carolina Assembly met in October, 1769, the Association had been pretty generally adopted by the other colonies; consequently, the action of North Carolina was awaited with some concern. The leaders of the Assembly realized the situation fully, and were by no means ready to go home until they had taken the necessary action to bring the colony in line with the Continental movement. Accordingly, immediately upon their dissolution, following the example of Virginia, they called

---

[1] Col. Rec., VIII, 121—124.

the members together in convention to "take measures for preserving the true and essential interests of the province." John Harvey was unanimously elected moderator. After discussing the situation fully through a session of two days, the convention agreed upon a complete non-importation program, and recommended it to their constituents in order to show their "readiness to join heartily with the other colonies in every legal method which may most probably tend to procure a redress" of grievances. This association was signed by sixty-four of "the late representatives of the people * * * being all that were then present." [1] Their names, unfortunately, are not recorded. When the policy of non-importation was tried in opposition to the Stamp Act it was not successful, and the Loyalists ridiculed the attempt of Virginia to revive it as a weapon against the Townshend Acts. But a new element had now entered into the situation: the union sentiment had developed into a reality, and the opponents of the government, taking advantage of this fact, pushed the movement with vigor and success. Colony after colony joined the movement, and when North Carolina came in, the Whig papers declared with great satisfaction: "This completes the chain of union throughout the continent for the measure of non-importation and economy." [2]

---

[1] South Carolina Gazette and Country Journal, December 8, 1769.
[2] Ibid.

But it was a simpler matter to adopt an association than to enforce it. The Tories, of course, opposed the whole scheme, and would gladly have welcomed an opportunity to defeat it. Their chance seemed to come when in April, 1770, Parliament repealed all the duties except the one on tea. The Tories hoped and the Whigs feared that this concession would break up the non-importation associations. While the former applauded the magnanimity of Parliament for yielding so much, the latter denounced the ministry for yielding no more, and regarding the partial repeal as a mere trap, redoubled their efforts to keep the association intact.

In North Carolina the merchants of the Cape Fear were the largest importers of British goods, and everybody recognized that their action would determine the matter. No non-importation association could be made effective without their cooperation. Fortunately, Cornelius Harnett, one of the chief merchants of the province, was also chairman of the Sons of Liberty, and his influence went far toward determining the course of the Cape Fear merchants. As soon as information of Parliament's action reached Wilmington, he called a meeting of the Sons of Liberty in the Wilmington District to take proper action. A large number of "the principal inhabitants" attended at Wilmington, June 2, and "unanimously agreed to keep strictly to the non-importation agreement," and to cooperate with the other colonies "in every legal measure for obtaining ample redress of the grievances so justly complained of." In order to make their resolution more effective, they chose a committee to consult upon such measures as would best evince their "patriotism and loyalty" to the common cause, and "manifest their unanimity with the rest of the colonies." This committee was composed of thirty members representing all the Cape Fear counties and the towns of Wilmington and Brunswick. Among its members were Cornelius Harnett, James Moore, Samuel Ashe, Richard Quince, and Farquard Campbell, the most prominent merchants and planters of the Cape Fear section. Cornelius Harnett was unanimously chosen chairman. They declared their intention to enforce strictly the non-importation association; denounced the merchants of Rhode Island "who contrary to their solemn and voluntary contract, have violated their faith pledged to the other colonies, and thereby shamefully deserted the common cause of American liberty"; declared that they would have no dealings with any merchant who imported goods "contrary to the spirit and intention" of the non-importation association; and constituted themselves a special committee to inspect all goods imported into the Cape Fear and to keep the public informed of any that were brought in contrary to the association. They then ordered their resolves to be "immediately transmitted to all the trading towns in this colony"; and in the spirit of co-operation, Cornelius Harnett wrote to the Sons of Liberty of South Carolina to inform them of their action. In this letter he said:

"We beg leave to assure you that the inhab-itants of those six counties and we doubt not of every county in this province, are convinced of the necessity of adhering to their former resolutions, and you may depend, they are tenacious of their just rights as any of their brethren on the continent and firmly resolved to stand or fall with them in support of the common cause of American liberty. Worthless men * * * are the production of every country, and we are also unhappy as to have a few among us 'who have not virtue enough to resist the allurement of present gain.' Yet we can venture to assert, that the people in general of this colony, will be spirited and steady in support of their rights as English subjects, and will not tamely submit to the yoke of oppression. 'But if by the iron hand of power,' they are at last crushed; it is however their fixed resolution, either to fall with the same dignity and spirit you so justly mention, or transmit to their posterity entire, the inestimable blessings of our free Constitution. The disinterested and public spirited behaviour of the merchants and other inhabitants of your colony justly merits the applause of every lover of liberty on the continent. The people of any colony who have not virtue enough to follow so glorious examples must be lost to every sense of freedom and consequently deserve to be slaves." [1]

The interchange of such views and opinions among the several colonies greatly strengthened the union sentiment; while the practical operation of the non-importation associations revealed to both the Americans and the ministry the power that lay in a united America.

In the meantime, while Cornelius Harnett and his colleagues were struggling with the authority of Parliament and bending all their energy toward the continental movement, dissensions in the interior counties of North Carolina came near to counteracting all the good results of their work. It must be assumed here that the reader is familiar with the history of the Regulators. The story has been told and retold with much feeling until it has become one of the most hotly controverted chapters in the history of North Carolina. The controversies, however, do not grow out of a difference of opinion relative to the facts. These are pretty well agreed upon, but from the same facts historians have drawn widely different conclusions. One sees in the

---

[1] South Carolina Gazette and Country Journal, July 5, 1770: July 26, 1770, and August 9, 1770.

Regulators a devoted band of patriots who fired the opening gun of the Revolution; the other sees a disorganized mob whose success would have resulted in anarchy. Here we are concerned only with the views of Cornelius Harnett and the other Revolutionary leaders.

Cornelius Harnett sympathized with the grievances of the Regulators. They were excessive taxes, extortionate fees, and dishonest officials. Neither Tryon nor the men who followed him denied that they had cause for complaint. In a message to the Assembly in December, 1770, excellent in style and admirable in spirit, Tryon recommended the most scrupulous inquiries into the complaints against the public officials and the redress of those which had an existence.[1] A few days later Cornelius Harnett, chairman of the committee on propositions and grievances, reported as the opinion of the committee that officers who exacted greater fees than the law allowed were guilty of a very great grievance; that the acceptance of fees by members of the Assembly for securing the passage of private bills was illegal; and that the custom which had grown up in the courts of prosecuting principal debtors and their securities, when all the parties were living, in different actions though bound in one specialty, was a great grievance that tended only to increase the fees of attorneys, clerks, sheriffs and other officials. He therefore

---

[1] Col. Rec., VIII, 282.

recommended the passage of an act plainly ascertaining what fees the officers were entitled to receive.[1] The Assembly appeared to be so ready to listen to the complaints of the Regulators that James Iredell declared that a majority of the House were of regulating principles, and had not only determined on a leveling plan, but would be very reluctant to pass any law for a spirited vindication of the honor of the government. It seems clear that legal remedies would have been provided for their grievances had the Regulators been willing to wait upon the slow process of lawmaking. That the law needed amendment was not denied, but the Assembly wisely thought that hasty and ill considered changes would likely produce more and greater evils than they removed. Reformers rarely take this fact into consideration; they see only the evil which they wish to remove and, intent upon that, are blind to the other, and sometimes greater evils into which their plans would lead. The reformer is by nature a radical, the lawmaker is, or ought to be a conservative, and when he does not move fast enough for the reformer, the reformer becomes impatient and is more than likely to run into excesses in words or deeds. So it was with the Regulators. Impatience at what they thought the indifference of the colonial government to their grievances led them into excesses which not even their warmest

[1] Col. Rec., VIII, 388—89.

sympathizers can condone. For, to break into courts of justice, driving judges from the bench; to "tear down justice from her tribunal," and insultingly to set up mock courts filling the records with billingsgate and profanity; to drag unoffending attorneys through the streets at the peril of their lives, and wantonly to assault peaceful citizens for refusing to sympathize with lawlessness,—these are not proper methods of redressing grievances, however oppressive, in a civilized community under a government based upon the will of the people.

Such were the methods that lost the Regulators the sympathy and support of Cornelius Harnett and his colleagues, and compelled both the king's governor and the people's Assembly to look less to the redress of grievances than to the suppression of anarchy. Harnett in the report already quoted declared that the Regulators by obstructing the sheriffs in the collection of public taxes and by the many outrages and riotous proceedings in opposition to the courts of justice which they had committed, were guilty of a real grievance, detrimental to the good order of society, and manifestly tending to distress the peaceable and loyal subjects of the province who were compelled to pay taxes for the support of the government: and he recommended that the ringleaders of the insurgents be compelled by law to answer for their conduct and prevented from committing such outrages in the future. A committee of which Harnett, and other Revolutionary patriots, were members drafted a message to the governor, which was adopted by the Assembly, denouncing the "daring and insolent attack" of the Regulators on the court at Hillsboro; declaring that their "dissolute principles and licentious spirit" rendered them too formidable for the ordinary process of the law; and recommending the adoption of "measures at once spirited and decisive."[1] The measure adopted was introduced by Samuel Johnston and is known as the "Johnston Act." It was undoubtedly an unwise and excessively severe law. As has been truly said: "It is doubtful if so drastic a measure ever passed an[other] American Assembly"; but the Assembly felt, as James Iredell said, commenting on it, that "desperate diseases must have desperate remedies."[2]

It is not difficult to understand the feelings of the leaders in the Assembly. They were keenly aware of the injury the conduct of the Regulators would do to the American cause in England. Though the opposition to the Stamp Act and the Townshend Acts had been firm and decided, it had been carried on peaceably and orderly: yet the Americans had been freely denounced in England as lawless and violent men, delighting

[1] Col. Rec., VIII, 311—313.
[2] Col. Rec.,VIII, 270.

in riot and rebellion.   They had found it by no
means the easiest part of their work to counteract
this view even among those who wished them well.
The proceedings of the Regulators, when reported
to the home government, could not fail to give
to their enemies a decided advantage, for the
people of the mother country would draw no
distinction between the Sons of Liberty on the
Cape Fear and the Regulators on the Eno.   All
would be classed as rebellious subjects who
deserved punishment.   It was doubtless the
realization of this fact that induced the Assembly
to adopt such a drastic policy toward the Regulators.

Cornelius Harnett was in thorough sympathy
with this policy and when Tryon marched to Alamance, Harnett marched with him to give his
support to the expedition which he had urged
the governor to make.   He served as a volunteer
holding neither military rank nor civil office, but
his services were of such value that the Assembly
gave them special recognition.   In December,
1771, the House "taking into consideration the account of Mr. Cornelius Harnett in the late expedition against the insurgents and fully convinced
of the great service rendered his country by his
zeal and activity therein," voted to allow him £100
"to defray the extraordinary expenses he was at in
that service."   When this resolution was received
in the Council that body expressed pleasure

at the opportunity of showing its appreciation of Harnett's "merit and good services." But when the Council requested that for similar services a similar recognition be given to Samuel Cornell, a member of the Council, the other House declined, explaining that the allowance to Harnett was made not only because his services entitled him to the notice of the Assembly, but also because he had not been in any office or employment from which he could possibly derive any compensation for the great expenses he had incurred in that expedition. This explanation satisfied the Council and the resolution was adopted. [1]

But the question arises, Did the Regulators begin the Revolution and at Alamance shed the first blood in the cause of independence? As we answer this question we must condemn or commend the attitude of Cornelius Harnett toward them. The Regulators made no such claim for themselves: on the contrary when an opportunity was offered to fight for independence they arrayed themselves against it. The oath which Tryon compelled them to take after the battle of Alamance is pleaded as sufficient explanation of their course during the Revolution; but every American who pleaded the cause or fought the battles of independence had repeatedly taken a similar oath. There is a fundamental difference, which Dr. Bassett points out, between

---

[1] Col. Rec., IX, 195—205.

the Regulation and the Revolution.[1] The Regulators were not contending for a great constitutional principle lying at the very foundation of human government such as inspired the men who fought the Revolution. Every grievance of which the former complained could have been removed by their own representatives in an Assembly freely chosen by the people; the American people sent no representatives to the British Parliament. The former, therefore, resisted oppressive methods of administering laws passed by their own representatives; the latter, it need scarcely be said, revolted against taxation without representation. The one was an insurrection, the other a revolution. The distinction is plain and goes to the root of the whole matter. A revolution involves a change of principles in government and is constitutional in its significance; an insurrection is an uprising of individuals to prevent the execution of laws and aims at a change of agents who administer, or the manner of administering affairs under forms or principles that remain intact. There is of course all the difference in the world between the two. It is this difference, for instance, that raises the resistance to the Stamp Act on the Cape Fear far above the revolt of the Regulators in dignity and significance, and elevates the

---

[1] "The Regulators of North Carolina": Report of the American Historical Association, 1894, 141—212.

5

former but not the latter above the level of a
riot. The Americans denied the validity of
the Stamp Act because in passing it Parliament,
as they thought, assumed to itself an authority
which it did not rightfully possess, and thus
undermined their constitutional liberties. The
Regulators did not dispute the constitutional
right of the Assembly to enact the laws of which
they complained; they objected to the improper
execution of those laws. The principles of the
former contest did not die with the repeal of
the Stamp Act, but became the living issues in
the great Revolution. The movement of the
Regulators expended itself at Alamance and
died out with the removal of the causes which
gave rise to it. However just the cause of the
Regulators may have been, it did not involve
a vital principle of political freedom, and it seems
clear that it is a total misconception of the real
significance of the American Revolution to call
Alamance the first battle in the cause of independence.

Cornelius Harnett understood this. He was
too clear-sighted and practical a statesman not
to see that the movement of the Regulators
was antagonistic to the continental movement
against the encroachments of the British Parliament. He "had neither the mind of a visionary
nor the temper of an insurrectionist. * * * He
saw clearly that the Regulators were held together

not by the cohesion of principle but merely by a common hatred of government officials and a determination to wreak vengeance upon them. No man felt more keenly than Harnett the difference between liberty and license." It was for him and the "other far-sighted leaders who rallied around him" to show "to the world that the Revolution in North Carolina was to be led by men who knew as by instinct the difference between lawlessness and self-government, who had weighed the questions at issue in the scale of pure principle, and who ceased to be loyal to England only that they might pledge undying loyalty to the spirit of liberty."[1] Liberty regulated by law was the goal at which they aimed. When the tyranny of a king threatened the one, and when the anarchy of a mob endangered the other, Cornelius Harnett was equally ready to sacrifice himself and his fortune in resistance.

[1] Smith: U. N. C. Mag., May, 1907, 387—88.

V

COMMITTEES OF CORRESPONDENCE

Soon after his victory at Alamance, Tryon left North Carolina for New York. He was succeeded by Josiah Martin. Martin, as Saunders observes, was a man ill calculated to conduct an administration successfully even in ordinary times. Stubborn and tactless, obsequious to those in authority and overbearing to those under authority, he found himself suddenly placed in a position that required almost every quality of mind and character that he did not possess. He was, it is true, an honest man, but he was intolerant and knew nothing of the art of diplomacy. Sincerely devoted to the king, whom he thought it no degradation to regard literally as a master, he had no faith in the sincerity of the Americans when in one breath they declared their loyalty to the Crown and in the next demanded from the Crown a recognition of their constitutional rights. "Insufferably tedious and turgid, his dispatches make the tired reader long for the well-constructed, clear-cut sentences and polished impertinences of Tryon,"[1] and show that he was utterly incapable of understanding the people whom he had been sent to rule. No worse selection could have been made at that time; the people of North Carolina

---

[1] Col. Rec., Prefatory Notes, IX, iii—iv.

were in no mood to brook the petty tyranny of a provincial governor, and Martin's personality became one of the chief factors that drove North Carolina headlong into revolution and prepared the colony, first of all the colonies, to take a definite stand for independence.

Their experience with the Stamp Act and the Townshend Act, taught the king and ministry the power that lay in a united America, and henceforth they avoided as far as possible such measures as would give the colonies a common grievance upon which they could unite. Their change of policy embraced two principles which the Americans promptly repudiated. One was the principle of the Declaratory Act. The other was the assumption that the king's instructions to the provincial governors were of higher authority than acts of assemblies and were binding on both assemblies and governors. For the next three years these instructions "played an important part in American politics. * * * They came under the king's sign manual, with the privy seal annexed. It was said that officials could not refuse to execute them without giving up the rights of the Crown. A set was not framed to apply to all the colonies alike, but special instructions were sent to each colony as local circumstances dictated. Hence the patriots could not create a general issue on them." [1]   The Americans at once perceived their danger, and were

[1] Frothingham: "The Rise of the Republic of the United States," 252.

not to be caught in the trap; for when they came
a few years later to adopt a Declaration of
Independence, this policy of the king was one
of the "facts submitted to a candid world,"
in justification of their action.

In North Carolina the issue was raised between
the governor and the Assembly over the financial
policy of the province, and over the location
of the boundary line between North Carolina
and South Carolina; but the decisive battle
against royal instructions was fought over
the Assembly's efforts to frame a court-law.
The point at issue was the "foreign attachment
clause." British merchants who transacted business in the province through agents without
ever being here in person, became in course of
time extensive landowners here. The Tryon
court-law contained a clause empowering the
colonial courts to attach this property for debts
owed by such merchants to North Carolinians.
The merchants objected to the clause, but the
king refused to veto the act because by its own
provision it was to expire at the end of five years
and he expected, when a new bill was framed,
to have the clause omitted without interfering
with the business of the courts. Accordingly
he instructed Governor Martin not to pass any
bill containing the attachment clause.[1]

The struggle began in the Assembly of January,
1773, and during that and the next two sessions

---

[1] Col. Rec., IX, 235—36.

was the occasion of one of the best conducted
debates in the history of the colonial Assembly. [1]
Both sides maintained their positions with ability.
On the part of the Assembly William Hooper
and Samuel Johnston, both lawyers, Robert
Howe and Cornelius Harnett, both laymen,
bore the brunt of the battle.   On the other side
the governor was ably supported by the Council.
The Council declined to pass the Assembly's
bill unless it was so amended as to provide that
attachment proceedings should be "according
to the laws and statutes of England." [2]   But the
Assembly reminded the Council that in England
such proceedings existed by municipal custom,
not by statute, and were "so essentially local"
in their application "as not to admit of being
extended by any analogy to this province."
They contended that "to secure a privilege so
important the mode of obtaining it should be
grounded in certainty, the law positive and
express, and nothing left to the exercise of doubt
or discretion." [3]   They therefore rejected the
Council's amendment.   After much debate a
compromise was effected by the addition of a
clause suspending the operation of the act until
the king's pleasure could be learned.   The
Assembly thereupon sent it to their agent with
instructions to leave no stone unturned to secure

---

[1] The proceedings of these assemblies are printed in the Colonial
Records of North Carolina, IX, 376—591, 706—788, 831—950.

[2] Col. Rec., IX, 427.

[3] Col. Rec., IX, 558—560

the royal signature. He was to say to the king that "so important does this matter appear to this province that they can not by any means think of giving it up, * * * choosing rather the misfortune of a temporary deprivation of laws than to form any system whereby they may be left without remedy on this great point."[1]

To this appeal the king replied by rejecting the bill and instructing Governor Martin to create courts of oyer and terminer by the exercise of the "ever ready prerogative." Thus another element of discord was injected into the controversy, for when the Assembly met in December, the governor was compelled to inform them of the "royal disallowance" of the court-law, and at the same time to ask for money to meet the expenses of his prerogative courts. The Assembly's refusal was sharp and peremptory. They declared that while "one of the greatest calamities to which any political society can be liable," the suspension of the judicial powers of the government, had befallen the province, and no hope of redress through "the interposition of government" remained, "yet the misery of such a situation vanishes in competition with a mode of redress exercised by courts unconstitutionally framed: it is the blessed distinction of the British code of laws that our civil and criminal jurisdiction have their foundation in the laws of the land, and are regulated

---

[1] Col. Rec., IX, 578—580.

by principles as fixed as the Constitution. We humbly conceive that the power of issuing commissions of oyer and terminer and general gaol delivery, delegated by his Majesty to your Excellency, can not be legally carried into execution without the aid of the legislature of this province, and that we can not consistent with the justice due to our constituents make provision for defraying the expense attending a measure which we do not approve." [1]

The governor and his Council protested, argued, pleaded, and threatened. The Council predicted that unless courts were speedily established the "province must soon be deserted by its inhabitants and an end put to its *name* and *political* existence," and reproached the House for bringing the colony to this distressed situation "for the sake only of a comparatively small advantage supposed to lie in a mode of proceeding by attachment, a proceeding unknown both to the common and statute law of the mother country." [2] This message drew fire from the House. The issue now involved much more than a mere legal procedure; the independence of the Assembly as a legislative body was at stake. Was the Assembly, in the future, to be a lawmaking body, representing the people, or a mere machine for registering the will of the sovereign? "Appointed by the people," retorted

---

1 Col. Rec., IX, 742—743.
2 Col. Rec., IX, 768—770.

the House, "to watch over their rights and privileges, and to guard them from every encroachment of a private and public nature, it becomes our duty and will be our constant endeavor to preserve them secure and inviolate to the present age, and to transmit them unimpaired to posterity. * * * The rules of right and wrong, the limits of the prerogative of the Crown and of the privileges of the people are, in the present refined age, well known and ascertained; to exceed either of them is highly unjustifiable. Were the attachment law as formerly enjoyed by us as small an advantage * * * as you contend it is, the right we possess to that is equal to the rights to a more important object; in the smallest, it [a surrender of the right] is bartering the rights of a people for a present convenience, in a greater, it would be the same crime aggravated only by its circumstances. We observe with surprise that a doctrine maintained by a former House of Assembly is now adopted by you, and that you disclose as your opinion that attachments are not known to the common or statute law of England; what then did government tender to this people in lieu of their former mode, when it proffered to the last Assembly *a mode of attachment agreeable to the laws of England?"* [1]

Finding appeals to loyalty and threats of punishment equally unavailing, and caught in

1 Col. Rec., IX, 779—782.

his inconsistency, the governor determined to send the members home to consult their constituents, and accordingly sent his private secretary to command the House to attend him at the Palace. Knowing well enough what this meant, the House took a parting shot well calculated to ruffle his spirits. A committee was appointed to draw an address to the king, and was instructed "as the most effectual means to promote its success," to request Governor Tryon, "who happily for this country for many years presided over it, and of whose good intentions to its welfare we feel the fullest convictions," to forward it to his Majesty and support it "with his interest and influence." He was asked to "accept of this important trust as testimony of the great affection this colony bears him, and the entire confidence they repose in him." The members of the committee to prepare this address were Harvey, Johnston, Howe, Ashe, Hooper, Hewes, Isaac Edwards and Harnett.[1] After adopting this insulting resolution as much to show their contempt for Martin as their regard for Tryon, the members of the House proceeded to the Palace where they were dismissed.

But it was useless for the governor to appeal from the Assembly to the people; it was but an appeal from the teachers to the taught. To send the former back to their constituents was but to send them to gather fresh endorsements

---

[1] Col. Rec., IX, 786—787.

and receive renewed support in their contest. When they returned in March, 1774, Cornelius Harnett, who reported the Assembly's reply to the governor's message, told the governor that they had consulted the people, had stated to them candidly the point for which they contended, and had informed them how far the king was disposed to indulge their wishes. "These facts," he declared, "we have represented to them fairly, disdaining any equivocation or reserve that might leave them ignorant of the conduct we have pursued or the real motives that influenced it. And we have the heartfelt satisfaction to inform your Excellency that they have expressed their warmest approbation of our past proceedings, and have given us positive instructions to persist in our endeavours to obtain the process of foreign attachments upon the most liberal and ample footing."[1] To this message the governor replied in one of his few really good papers. He wrote with conflicting feelings for he was compelled to defend an instruction of his master with which he did not entirely sympathize. Passing by the "just exultation" with which the Assembly told him of their constituents' approval of their course, he made an eloquent plea for compromise.[2] But the Assembly stood firm, passed the usual bill with the usual clause, and, declaring that they had

---

[1] Col. Rec., IX, 879—880.
[2] Col. Rec., IX, 890—893.

pursued every measure to relieve the colony from its distressed condition, sent it to the governor. The governor rejected it. This brought the struggle to an end for the only other Assembly that met in North Carolina under royal rule was in session but four stormy days and did not have time to consider the court-law. North Carolina, therefore, remained without courts for the trial of civil causes until after independence was declared; and among the causes recited in the Declaration of Independence to justify that action, was the following: "He [the king] has obstructed the administration of justice, by refusing his assent to laws for establishing judiciary powers."

The situation in North Carolina was indeed serious. In March, 1773, Josiah Quincy, Jr., of Boston, traveling through the province, noted that but five provincial laws were in force, that no courts were open, that no one could recover a debt except for small sums within the jurisdiction of a magistrate's court, and that offenders escaped with impunity. "The people," he declared, "are in great consternation about the matter; what will be the result is problematical." [1] Many were disposed to charge the whole trouble to the governor. They did not believe that he had "properly or judiciously explained to the government at home" the necessity for the protection they sought; and

---

[1] Memoir of the Life of Josiah Quincy, Jr., 117 et seq.

they charged to his "spirit of intolerance and impatience" the failure of the Assembly to pass a county court-law, "the jurisdiction of which would have been so limited that it could not possibly have operated to the disfavor of any British merchant," and the want of which subjected the people of the province to innumerable inconveniences. [1] But there was no disposition on the part of the Whig leaders to shirk their own responsibility. Fortunately they received loyal support from their constituents, who chose rather to bear all the inconveniences of the situation than to surrender the independence of their judiciary. The royal government was thoroughly beaten because the people made anarchy tolerable.

The Whig leaders saw through the policy of the king in trying to avoid a general issue, and held many an anxious conference to devise a working plan for united action. One of the most important, as it was one of the most interesting of these conferences, was held between Josiah Quincy, Jr., of Massachusetts, and Cornelius Harnett, of North Carolina, at the home of the latter on the Cape Fear. Quincy arrived at Brunswick March 26, and spent the next five days enjoying the hospitality of the Cape Fear patriots. He found William Hill "warmly attached to the cause of American freedom";

---

[1] "A portrait of North Carolina" by "A Freeholder," in the Cape Fear Mercury February, 23, 1774, copied in the South Carolina Gazette and Country Journal, March 14, 1774.

William Dry "seemingly warm against the measures of British and continental administration"; William Hooper "apparently in the Whig interest." The night of March 30th he spent at the home of Cornelius Harnett. Here all doubt of his host's political sentiments vanished. "Spent the night," he records, "at Mr. Harnett's, the Samuel Adams of North Carolina (except in point of fortune.) Robert Howe Esq., Harnett and myself made the social triumvirate of the evening. The plan of continental correspondence highly relished, much wished for, and resolved upon as proper to be pursued." Tradition affirms that Quincy, delighted at finding Harnett's views coinciding so entirely with his own, was unable to refrain from giving his host a cordial embrace. Both esteemed the opportunity for further conference of such importance that Quincy remained with Harnett through the next day and night.[1]

No other man whom he met in his travels, seems to have made such a strong impression on Quincy as Harnett. Though he talked and dined and wined with the leading men in the southern and middle colonies, "he nowhere else likens any one to his beau-ideal, Samuel Adams." At that time Adams was probably the most influential political personality on the continent. Quincy was one of his "foster children"; perhaps

[1] Memoir of the Life of Josiah Quincy, Jr., 120.

his most intimate political follower. His conference with Harnett, therefore, was almost like a personal conference between Samuel Adams, the pioneer of independence in the North, and Cornelius Harnett, the pioneer of independence in the South.

The "plan of continental correspondence" was, of course, original with neither Quincy nor Harnett. Samuel Adams had already put a system of provincial correspondence into operation in Massachusetts; and a few days before Quincy reached North Carolina, but too late for the news to have reached Wilmington, the Virginia Assembly had proposed to the other assemblies the organization of a system of inter-colonial committees to carry on a "continental correspondence." During the summer several of the colonies adopted the plan. The decision of North Carolina had been practically settled at Wilmington in March, but as the Assembly did not meet until December, no committee was appointed. On the second day of the session, John Harvey, the speaker, laid the Virginia resolutions before the House; and Howe, Harnett and Johnston were appointed a committee to draw an answer. In their report they recommended hearty concurrence in the "spirited resolves" of the Virginia Assembly, and the appointment of a committee of correspondence to consist of Harvey, Howe, Harnett,

Hooper, Caswell, Edward Vail, Ashe, Hewes and
Johnston.[1] The work of this committee bore
good fruit, for the members brought to their
task a truly national spirit in dealing with continental affairs. To use a modern political
term, they adopted a platform in which they
declared that the inhabitants of all the colonies
"ought to consider themselves interested in
the cause of the town of Boston as the cause
of America in general"; that they would "concur
with and cooperate in such measures as may be
concerted and agreed on by their sister colonies"
for resisting the measures of the British ministry,
and that in order to promote "conformity and
unanimity in the councils of America," a Continental Congress was "absolutely necessary."[2]
The significance of this system of committees
was soon apparent. Indeed, as John Fiske
declares, it "was nothing less than the beginning
of the American union. * * * It only remained
for the various inter-colonial committees to as-
semble together, and there would be a congress
speaking in the name of the continent."[3]

The suggestion for such a congress followed
immediately and instantly found favor. It
was intended that the delegates should be chosen
by the assemblies. In North Carolina, Governor
Martin, after the stormy session of March, 1774,

[1] Col. Rec., IX, 740—741.
[2] State Records, XI, 245—248.
[3] The American Revolution, I, 81.

6

made up his mind to follow the example of Tryon and do without an assembly until he saw a chance for a better one. But Martin lacked a good deal of Tryon's shrewdness and popularity, and the men who led the Assembly were not the kind to be caught twice in the same trap. When the governor's secretary communicated this purpose to John Harvey, Harvey, "in a very violent mood" exclaimed: "In that case the people will call an assembly independent of the governor." He determined to issue over his own name a call for a provincial congress, and those whom he consulted expressed their approval.[1] It was thought better, however, for the call to proceed from some other source, so a mass meeting at Wilmington launched the movement July 21;[2] and on August 25, seventy-one delegates from thirty-six counties and towns met in convention at New Bern.[3] Cornelius Harnett spent the summer of 1774 in the North and, therefore, was not a member of this Congress. The Congress gave expression to the American position on the issues in dispute with the mother country in a series of spirited and clear-cut resolutions; declared for a Continental Congress, and elected Hooper, Hewes and Caswell delegates. John Harvey, the moderator, was authorized to call another Congress whenever he deemed it necessary.

---

[1] Col. Rec., IX, 968.
[2] Col. Rec., IX, 1016.
[3] Col. Rec., IX, 1041—1049.

No more significant step had ever been taken in North Carolina than the successful meeting of this Congress. It revealed the people to themselves. They began to understand that there was no peculiar power in the writs and proclamations of a royal governor; they themselves could elect delegates and organize legislatures without the intervention of a king's authority, and this was a long step toward independence.

Seeing that he was beaten, Martin determined to make the best of a bad situation, and called an assembly to meet at New Bern, April 4, 1775. John Harvey promptly called a congress to meet at. the same place, April 3. Of the two bodies the Congress was the larger, but as a rule the members of the Assembly were also members of the Congress. Cornelius Harnett represented his old constituents in both bodies. The governor was furious and denounced Harvey's action in a resounding proclamation. The Congress replied by electing Harvey moderator, and the Assembly by electing him speaker. The governor roundly scored both bodies, and both bodies roundly scored the governor. It was, indeed, a pretty situation. One set of men composed two assemblies, one legal, sitting by authority of the royal governor and in obedience to his writ; the other illegal, sitting in defiance of his authority and in disobedience of his proclamation. The governor impotently called on the former to join him in dispersing the latter. The two assemblies met in the same hall and were presided over by the same man.[1] "When the governor's private secretary was announced at the door, in an instant, in the twinkling of an eye, Mr. Moderator Harvey * * * would become Mr. Speaker Harvey * * * and gravely receive his Excellency's message."[2]

Neither body accomplished much. The Congress approved the Continental Association adopted by the Continental Congress and recommended it to the people of the province; thanked their delegates to the Continental Congress for their services and reelected them; and authorized John Harvey, or in the event of his death, Samuel Johnston, to call another congress when necessary, and then adjourned *sine die*. The Assembly had but time to organize and exchange messages with the governor when it too came to an end. The first offense was the election of John Harvey speaker. The governor winced at this, but held his peace. "The manner, however, of my admitting him," he wrote, "I believe, sufficiently testified my disapprobation of his conduct while it marked my respect for the election of the House." The second day the House offended again by inviting the delegates to the Congress, who were not also members of the Assembly, to join in the latter's deliberations.

[1] Col. Rec., IX, 1125, 1145, 1177, 1178—1185, 1187—1205.
[2] Col. Rec., Prefatory Notes, IX, xxxiv.

The governor promptly issued his proclamation forbidding this unholy union, but "not a man obeyed it." On the fourth day the House adopted resolutions approving the Continental Association, thanking the delegates to the Continental Congress for their services, and endorsing their election. This was more than Martin had bargained for; his wrath boiled over, and on April 8, 1775, he issued his proclamation dissolving the Assembly. Thus he put an end to the last Assembly that ever sat in North Carolina at the call of a royal governor, and by its dissolution brought British rule in that province to a close forever.

VI
COMMITTEES OF SAFETY

In order to provide an executive authority to enforce its policy, the Congress of August, 1774, recommended that "a committee of five persons be chosen in each county" for that purpose.[1] The Continental Congress in October recommended a similar system throughout the thirteen colonies. In North Carolina the plan as finally worked out contemplated one committee in each of the towns, one in each of the counties, one in each of the six military districts, and one for the province at large. In all our history there has been nothing else like these committees. Born of necessity, originating in the political and economic confusion of the time, they touched the lives of the people in their most intimate affairs, and gradually extended their jurisdiction until they assumed to themselves all the functions of government. They enforced with vigor the resolves of the Continental and Provincial Congresses, some of which were most exacting in their demands and burdensome in their effects. They conducted inquiries into the actions and opinions of individuals, and not only "determined what acts and opinions constituted a man an enemy of his country, but passed upon his guilt or innocence, and fixed his punishment." They

[1] Col. Rec., IX, 1047.

raised money by fines and assessments for the purchase of gunpowder, arms, and all the other implements of war. The militia had to be enlisted, organized, equipped and drilled. In short, a revolution had to be inaugurated and it fell to these committees to do it. "Usurping some new authority every day, executive, judicial or legislative, as the case might be, their powers soon became practically unlimited." Governor Martin characterized them as "extraordinary tribunals." In every respect they were extraordinary, insurrectionary, revolutionary. Illegally constituted, they assumed such authority as would not have been tolerated in the royal government, and received such obedience as the king with all his armies could not have exacted. Yet not only did they not abuse their power, they voluntarily resigned it when the public welfare no longer needed their services. They were the offspring of misrule and rose and fell with their parent.

The most active and effective of these committees were those of Wilmington and New Hanover. Of these Cornelius Harnett was the master-spirit. When the Wilmington committee was organized, November 23, 1774, though he was then absent from the province, he was unanimously elected chairman. When the New Hanover county committee was organized, January 4, 1775, "to join and cooperate with the committee of the town," he was promptly placed at the head of the joint committee. The people were fully alive to the importance of the step they took in organizing these committees. The men whom they selected represented the wealth, the intelligence and the culture of the community. They were men of approved character and ability. Some of them afterwards achieved eminence in the history of North Carolina. Seldom have men entrusted with such extensive authority fulfilled their trust with greater fidelity. They discharged every duty with firmness and patience, with prudence and wisdom, and in the interest of the public welfare. From the first, we are told, Cornelius Harnett was "the very soul of the enterprise," "the life-breathing spirit of liberty among the people," possessing their confidence "to an extent that seems incredible." [1] Archibald Maclaine Hooper says: "The first motions of disaffection on the Cape Fear were prompted by him. When the conjunction favorable for his projects arrived, he kept concealed behind the curtain, while the puppets of the drama were stirred by his wires into acts of turbulence and disloyalty. Afterwards when a meeting was convened at Wilmington, he was bold in the avowal of his sentiments and in the expression of his opinions." As chairman of the joint committee, by his activity in "warning and watching the disaffected, encouraging the timid, collecting the means of defense, and com-

---

[1] U. N. C. Mag., IV, 136.

municating its enthusiasm to all orders," he made this local committee the most effective agency, except the Congress itself, in getting the Revolution under way in North Carolina. Governor Martin recognized in him the chief source of opposition to the royal government; and the Provincial Congress demanded his services for the province at large. When the Provincial Council was created Harnett was unanimously elected president, a position that made him in all but name the first chief executive of the newborn State. The work of this Council, too, was largely his work, and its success is proof of the ability which he brought to his task.

The policy of the Continental Congress aimed to promote economy and industry, to discourage extravagance and luxury, and to enforce the non-importation and non-exportation associations. Upon the committees of safety fell the task of making this policy effective.[1] It was neither an easy nor an agreeable task, for some features of the policy were extremely irritating in their operation and at times produced restlessness among the people. It required as much tact as determination for the committees to execute their orders with vigor without at the same time losing the support of their constit-

[1] The proceedings of the Wilmington-New Hanover committees may be found in the Colonial Records, vol. IX, pp. 1088, 1095, 1098, 1101, 1107, 1108, 1118, 1120, 1122, 1126, 1127, 1135, 1143, 1149, 1166, 1168, 1170, 1185, 1222, 1265, 1285; vol. X, pp. 12, 15, 24, 50, 64, 65, 68, 72, 87, 89, 91, 93, 112, 116, 121, 124, 141, 151, 157, 158, 220, 262, 263, 279, 282, 298, 304, 328, 331, 334, 335, 336, 345, 348, 363, 388, 389, 393, 405, 410, 411, 418, 421, 425, 431, 435, 477.

uents. In this double task the committees of Wilmington and New Hanover met with a remarkable degree of success. Though they enforced strictly the resolve against "expensive diversions and entertainments," interfering with horse-races, billiards, dancing and other pleasures, the people submitted without complaint. "Nothing," declared the committee, "will so effectively tend to convince the British Parliament that we are in earnest in opposition to their measures, as a voluntary relinquishment of our favorite amusements. * * * Many will cheerfully part with part of their property to secure the remainder. He only is the determined patriot who willingly sacrifices his pleasures on the altar of freedom." They seized and sold large quantities of goods imported contrary to the association. "The safety of the people is, or ought to be, the supreme law," wrote a merchant whose goods were seized; "the gentlemen of the committee will judge whether this law, or any act of Parliament, should, at this particular time, operate in North Carolina." Several planters who thought upon one pretext or another to get around the resolve forbidding the importation of slaves, were promptly summoned before the committee to "give a particular account" of their conduct, and as promptly required to re-ship their negroes by the first opportunity. The non-exportation resolve became operative September 10, 1775. A few merchants having conceived a scheme to circumvent the resolve through a technicality, were at once summoned before the committee who, determined to enforce the spirit as well as the letter of the resolve, effectively put an end to their scheme. When Parliament, in an effort to break up the Continental Association, passed an act "to restrain the trade and commerce" of certain colonies, from which North Carolina and some others were excepted, the Wilmington-New Hanover committees, at a large meeting over which Cornelius Harnett presided, "resolved, unanimously, that the exception of this colony, and some others, out of the said act, is a mean and base artifice, to seduce them into a desertion of the common cause of America"; and accordingly determined "that we will not accept of the advantages insidiously thrown out by the said act, but will strictly adhere to such plans as have been, and shall be, entered into by the Honorable Continental Congress, so as to keep up a perfect unanimity with our sister colonies." In their work the committees met with just enough opposition to enable them to make a display of firmness and determination. For instance, when Harnett at the head of the committee submitted to the people of Wilmington a test pledging the signers to "observe strictly" the Continental Association, eleven prominent men refused to sign.

They were promptly ostracized as "unworthy
the rights of freemen and as inimical to the
liberties of their country"; and held up before
the public that they might be "treated with
the contempt they deserve." There were no
braver men than some of those thus cut off from
their fellows, but they could not stand out
against the open scorn of their neighbors; within
less than a week eight of their number gave way
and subscribed the test. The committee justified
their course as being "a cement of allegiance"
to the Crown and as "having a tendency to
promote a constitutional attachment for the
mother country."

But in May, 1775, the last bond of such allegiance was snapped, and the last sentiment of
such attachment destroyed, by news that came
from Massachusetts. American blood had been
shed on Lexington green. Through the colonies
expresses rode day and night, carrying the news
of Lexington, of the rising of the minute-men,
and of the retreat from Concord.[1] In no other
way did the committees of safety give a better
illustration of their usefulness than in the trans-
mission of this news. From colony to colony,
from town to town, from committee to committee,
they hurried it along. New York received the
dispatches at midday, New Brunswick at mid-
night. They aroused Princeton at 3 o'clock in
the morning. Trenton read them at daybreak,

---

[1] Col. Rec., IX, 1229—1239.

Philadelphia at noon. They reached Baltimore at bed-time, Alexandria at the breakfast hour. Three days and nights the express rode on, down the Potomac, across the Rappahannock, the York and the James, through scenes since made famous, and on to Edenton. Edenton received the dispatches at 9 a. m., May 4, and hurried them on to Bath with the injunction "to disperse the material passages through all your parts." Bath hastened them on to New Bern with a message to send them forward "with the utmost dispatch." "Send them on as soon as possible to the Wilmington committee," directed New Bern to Onslow. "Disperse them to your adjoining counties," echoed Onslow to Wilmington. At 3 o'clock p. m., May 8, the messenger delivered his dispatches to Cornelius Harnett. Delaying just long enough to make copies, Harnett urged him on to Brunswick. "If you should be at a loss for a horse or a man," he wrote to the Brunswick committee, "the bearer will proceed as far as the Boundary House. You will please direct Mr. Marion or any other gentleman to forward the packet immediately southward with the greatest possible dispatch." He had signed his name when, overcome with a rush of sudden emotion, he seized his pen and dashed off impulsively: "P. S. For God's sake send the man on without the least delay and write to Mr. Marion to forward it by night and

day." Thus the news was sped to the southward, inspiring the forward, stirring the backward,
and arousing the continent. The committees
made the most of their opportunity. Governor
Martin complained that the rebel leaders received
the news more than a month before he did, and
that he received it "too late to operate against
the infamous and false reports of that transaction
which were circulated to this distance from Boston
in the space of 12 or 13 days." The first impression took "deep root in the minds of the vulgar
here universally and wrought a great change in
the face of things, confirming the seditious in
their evil purposes, and bringing over vast numbers of the fickle, wavering and unsteady multitude to their party." [1]

The battle of Lexington was the beginning
of war. For this result the patriots of the Cape
Fear were not wholly unprepared. Recognizing
that the Cape Fear would be the scene of the
first armed conflict in North Carolina, the
committees, under the direction of Cornelius
Harnett, had made every effort to be ready for
"the worst contingencies." They required the
merchants to sell their gunpowder to the committees for the public use, they bought it from
other committees, imported it from other colonies,
and employed agents to manufacture it. They
hired men to mould bullets. They seized the
public arms, and they compelled every person

---

[1] Col. Rec., X, 44.

who owned more than one gun to surrender all
but one for the public service. They smuggled
arms and ammunition from other colonies and
the West Indies in such quantities that Governor
Martin "lamented that effectual steps have not
been taken to intercept the supplies of warlike
stores that * * * are frequently brought into
this colony"; and asked for three or four cruisers
to guard the coast, for the sloop stationed at
Fort Johnston "is not sufficient to attend to the
smugglers in this [Cape Fear] river alone."[1] The
Wilmington committee required "every white
man capable of bearing arms" to enlist in one
of the companies that had been organized; and
early in July, 1775, gave as one reason for a
provincial congress which Harnett, Ashe and
Howe urged Johnston to call, "that a number
of men should be raised and kept in pay for the
defense of the country."[2] Nor were the committees unmindful of the necessity of preparing the
minds of the people for war. In this respect,
too, success crowned their efforts. Even historians who think North Carolina did not give
"general and heroic support to the cause of independence," declare that at the outbreak of the
Revolution the people were "aroused to an
extraordinary degree of enthusiasm."[3] This
enthusiasm Governor Martin charged partic-

---

[1] Col. Rec., X, 233.

[2] Col. Rec., X, 92.

[3] Dodd : South Atlantic Quarterly, I, 156.

ularly to the committees over which Cornelius
Harnett presided. To Lord Dartmouth he
wrote that the people "freely talk of hostility
toward Britain in the language of aliens and
avowed enemies," and he attributed this spirit
to "the influence of the committees" which, he
said, "hath been so extended over the inhabitants of the lower part [Cape Fear section] of
this country, * * * and they are at this day
to the distance of an hundred miles from the
sea coast, so generally possessed with the spirit
of revolt" that "the authority, the edicts and
ordinances of congresses, conventions and committees are established supreme and omnipotent
by general acquiescence or forced submission,
and lawful government is completely annihi-
lated." [1] The records of the committees fully
bear out these statements.

The governor wrote these dispatches from Fort
Johnston at the mouth of the Cape Fear river
where, frightened from the Palace at New Bern by
the New Bern committee, he had taken refuge.
Reaching there June 2, he began to lay his schemes
for counteracting the influence of the committees.
His activity took the form of a resounding proclamation, in which he denounced the committees
and warned the people against them; of an
application to General Gage for a royal standard
around which the loyal and faithful might rally;
and of an elaborate plan for the organization of

---

[1] Col. Rec., X, 49, 232, 244.

the Highlanders and Regulators of the interior for military service. His plans were approved by the king who promised such assistance as might be necessary. They gave great alarm to the Whigs. "Our situation here is truly alarming," wrote the Wilmington committee; "the governor [is] collecting men, provisions, warlike stores of every kind, spiriting up the back country, and perhaps the slaves; finally strengthening the fort with new works in such a manner as may make the capture of it extremely difficult."[1] "Nothing," declared Harnett, "shall be wanting on our part to disconcert such diabolical schemes."[2] The committees kept such close watch over his movements that Martin declared no messenger or letter could escape them. They intercepted his dispatches, frustrated his plans, and in general made life so miserable for him that he bemoaned his situation as "most despicable and mortifying to any man of greater feelings than a stoic." "I daily see indignantly the sacred majesty of my royal master insulted, the rights of his crown denied and violated, his government set at naught and trampled upon, his servants of highest dignity reviled, traduced, abused, the rights of his subjects destroyed by the most arbitrary usurpations, and the whole constitution

---

[1] Col. Rec., X, 91.

[2] MS. letter in the library at "Hayes"; copy in the collections of the North Carolina Historical Commission.

7

unhinged and prostrate, and I live, alas! ingloriously only to deplore it."[1]

On June 20, the committees of the Wilmington District, in session at Wilmington, declared that the governor had "by the whole tenor of his conduct, since the unhappy disputes between Great Britain and the colonies, discovered himself to be an enemy to the happiness of this colony in particular, and to the freedom, rights and privileges of America in general."[2] Determined, therefore, to treat him as an enemy, the Wilmington committee passed an order forbidding any communications with him. Expulsion from the province was the logical result of this order, and the leaders were soon ready to take this step also. In a letter to Samuel Johnston, July 13, the Wilmington committee said: "We have a number of enterprising young fellows that would attempt to take the fort [Fort Johnston], but are much afraid of having their conduct disavowed by the convention."[3] But what these "enterprising young fellows" were afraid to attempt, Cornelius Harnett, John Ashe and Robert Howe made up their minds to do. Captain John Collet, the commander of the fort, felt all the professional soldier's contempt for the militia and all the Britisher's contempt for the provincials, and took no pains to conceal his feelings.[4]

---

[1] Col. Rec., X, 47.
[2] Col. Rec., X, 27.
[3] Col. Rec., X, 91.
[4] Col. Rec., X, 112—115, 235.

A long series of studied insults had exasperated the people of the Cape Fear against him, but they had borne them all patiently. But now news came that at Governor Martin's command, he was preparing the fort "for the reception of a promised reinforcement," the arrival of which would be the signal for the erection of the king's standard. The committee regarded this as a declaration of war, and "having taken these things into consideration, judged it might be of the most pernicious consequences to the people at large, if the said John Collet should be suffered to remain in the fort, as he might thereby have an opportunity of carrying his iniquitous schemes into execution." They accordingly called for volunteers to take the fort, and in response "a great many volunteers were immediately collected." [1]

The committee's preparations alarmed Governor Martin. Nobody realized better than he that the fort could not be held against a determined attack. Yet its defense was a matter of honor and its surrender would have a bad effect in the province. Besides it held artillery "considerable in value," with a quantity of movable stores and ammunition. "Its artillery which is heavy," wrote Martin, "might in the hands of the mob be turned against the king's ship, and so annoy her as to oblige her to quit her present station which is most convenient in all

---

[1] Col. Rec., X, 93, 113—114.

respects." Then, too, an unsuccessful defense
meant the capture of the governor himself. In
this perplexing situation, Martin decided to
remove the stores to a transport, to withdraw
the garrison, dismantle the fortifications, and
seek refuge on board the *Cruizer*.[1] Almost at
the very hour of his flight, Lord Dartmouth was
writing to him: "I hope his Majesty's government in North Carolina may be preserved, and
his governor and other officers not reduced to the
disgraceful necessity of seeking protection on
board the king's ships."[2]

Smarting keenly under his disgrace, Martin
hastened to put on record the punishment he
desired to inflict on those most responsible for
it. From the cabin of the *"Cruizer*, Sloop of
War, in Cape Fear River," July 16, he wrote
to Lord Dartmouth:

"Hearing of a proclamation of the king, pro-
scribing John Hancock and Samuel Adams of the
Massachusetts Bay, and seeing clearly that
further proscriptions will be necessary before
government can be settled again upon sure
foundations in America, I hold it my indispensable duty to mention to your Lordship Cornelius Harnett, John Ashe, Robert Howes[3] and
Abner Nash, as persons who have marked them-

---

[1] Col. Rec., X. 96—98.

[2] Col. Rec., X, 90.

[3] "Robert Howes," wrote Martin, "is commonly called Howe, he
having impudently assumed that name for some years past in affecta-
tion of the noble family that bears it, whose least eminent virtues have
ever been far beyond his imitation." Col. Rec., X, 98.

selves out as proper objects for such distinction in this colony by their unremitted labours to promote sedition and rebellion here from the beginnings of the discontents in America to this time, that they stand foremost among the patrons of revolt and anarchy." [1]

In the meantime 500 minute-men had rendezvoused at Brunswick and, learning that the governor had fled to the *Cruizer*, marched on the fort and applied the torch. Early in the morning of July 19, the governor was aroused from his quarters by the announcement that Fort Johnston was on fire. Hurrying to the deck he beheld the rapid spread of the flames as they reduced the fort to ashes. The "rabble," he wrote, burned several houses erected by Captain Collet, and thus, in the words of the Wilmington committee, "effectually dislodged that atrocious freebooter." [2] "Mr. John Ashe and Mr. Cornelius Harnett," wrote the enraged governor, "were ringleaders of this savage and audacious mob." [3]

[1] Col. Rec., X, 98.
[2] Col. Rec., X, 114.
[3] Col. Rec., X, 108—109.

VII

THE PROVINCIAL COUNCIL

Upon the adjournment of the second Provincial Congress, April 7, 1775, authority was given to John Harvey, or in the event of his death to Samuel Johnston, to call another congress whenever he thought it necessary. It became necessary sooner than was expected. The flight of the governor left the province without a government or a constitutional method of calling an assembly. The battle of Lexington, soon to be followed by the destruction of Fort Johnston, produced a state of war. Both sides, recognizing this fact, were straining every nerve to get ready for the conflict. The situation, therefore, called for a larger authority than had been granted to the committees. A new government had to be formed, a currency devised, an army organized, munitions of war collected, and a system of defense planned; and all these preparations had to be made with a view to continental as well as provincial affairs. The leaders of the Whig party on the Cape Fear were required daily to exercise authority and accept responsibilities that exceeded the powers granted them; and they realized earlier than their friends elsewhere the necessity for organizing a government that could act independently of the royal authority. Only a general congress could provide this government. Accordingly on May 31, 1775, Howe, Harnett and Ashe joined in a letter to Samuel Johnston,—Harvey having died a few days before—suggesting that he call a congress "as soon as possible."[1] Johnston, however, thought the suggestion premature, and was reluctant to take a step that would widen still further the breach with the royal government. But at his quiet home on the Albemarle, Johnston failed to appreciate the situation on the Cape Fear, where a state of war practically existed, and he hesitated. "I expect my conduct in not immediately calling a provincial congress," he wrote, "will be much censured by many, but being conscious of having discharged my duty according to my best judgment I shall be the better able to bear it."[2] The Cape Fear leaders became impatient. On June 29, Howe, Harnett and Ashe, wrote again to Johnston taking him to task for his delay. "The circumstances of the times," and "the expectations of the people," they thought, ought to determine his conduct.[3] The people, wrote the Wilmington committee, were "continually clamouring for a provincial convention. They hope everything from its immediate session, fear everything from its

---

[1] Col. Rec., IX, 1285.

[2] MS. letter in the library at "Hayes," copy in collections of the North Carolina Historical Commission.

[3] State Rec., XI, 255.

delay." [1] Thus pressed, Johnston yielded and issued his call for a congress to meet at Hillsboro, August 20.

Nothing shows the progress that had been made toward revolution during the year more clearly than the full attendance at this Congress.[2] Just a year, lacking but five days, had passed since the first Congress met at New Bern. Seventy-one delegates were present, while five counties and three towns were unrepresented. At the second Congress, April 3, 1775, there were sixty-eight delegates present, while nine counties and two towns were unrepresented. But at the Hillsboro Congress, of August, 1775, every county and every borough town was represented, and one hundred and eighty-four delegates were present. Cornelius Harnett, together with Archibald Maclaine, a lawyer of ability, an aggressive debater and a bold patriot, represented Wilmington. The Congress unanimously elected Samuel Johnston "president,"—a significant change in the title of the presiding officer. The delegates brought to their deliberations a spirit almost national. No such thing as a truly national spirit existed in America at that time, but the Hillsboro Congress approached it as nearly as any body that had yet assembled in the colonies. Throughout their proceedings, in their appeals to the people, in the organization

---

[1] Col. Rec., X, 91.

[2] The proceedings of this Congress are printed in the Colonial Records, X, 164—220.

of an army, and in the formation of a provisional government, the one clear note sounding above all others was "the common cause of America."

The two most important matters before the Congress were the organization of an army and the formation of a provisional government. "Our principal debates," wrote Johnston, "will be about raising troops." As a preliminary to this step, the Congress first issued what may not inaptly be called a declaration of war. They declared that whereas "hostilities being actually commenced in the Massachusetts Bay by the British troops under the command of General Gage; * * * And whereas His Excellency Governor Martin hath taken a very active and instrumental share in opposition to the means which have been adopted by this and the other United Colonies for the common safety, * * * therefore [resolved that] this colony be immediately put into a state of defense." Two regiments of 500 men each were ordered "as part of and on the same establishment with the continental army." Colonel James Moore was assigned to the command of the first, Colonel Robert Howe to the second. Both won military fame in the war that followed. Six regiments of 500 minutemen each, were ordered to be raised in the six military districts into which the province was divided. When called into active service these troops were to be under the same discipline as the

continental troops. In addition to these 4,000
troops, provision was made for a more effective
organization of the militia, and for the organization of independent companies. An issue of
$125,000 of currency was authorized for their
equipment.

To agree upon a plan of civil government was
a more difficult task than the organization of
the army. Most men will frankly confess their
ignorance of military matters, and willingly
submit to the opinions of experts, but no American
would consider himself loyal to the teachings
of the fathers were he to admit himself incapable
of manufacturing offhand a plan of civil government. Congress, therefore, found no lack of
plans and ideas. On August 24 a strong committee, of which Harnett's friend and colleague,
Archibald Maclaine, was made chairman, was
appointed to prepare a plan of government
made necessary by the "absence" of Governor
Martin. The committee reported September
10. The plan proposed and adopted by the
Congress continued the Congress as the supreme
branch of the government with a few changes
that will be noticed. The executive and judicial
authority was vested in a Provincial Council,
six district committees of safety, and the local
committees of safety.

Congress was to be the supreme power in the
province. Henceforth it was to meet annually

at such time and place as should be designated by the Provincial Council. Delegates were to be elected annually in October. Each county was to be entitled to five delegates, and each borough town to one. The privilege of suffrage was limited to freeholders. The members of Congress were to qualify by taking an oath, in the presence of three members of the Provincial Council, acknowledging allegiance to the Crown, denying the right of Parliament to levy internal taxes on the colonies, and agreeing to abide by the acts and resolutions of the provincial and continental congresses. Each county and each town was to have one vote in Congress. No constitutional limitation was placed on the authority of Congress, and as the supreme power in the province it could review the acts of the executive branches of the government.

The executive powers of the government were vested in the committees. The committees of the counties and towns were continued practically as they were. Some limitation was placed on their power by making their acts reviewable by the district committees with the right of appeal to the Provincial Council. They were empowered to make such rules and regulations as they saw fit for the enforcement of their authority, but they could not inflict corporal punishment except by imprisonment. Within their own jurisdictions, they were to execute the orders of the district committees and the Provincial Council. They were to enforce the Continental Association and the ordinances of the provincial and continental congresses. Each committee was required to organize a sub-committee of secrecy, intelligence and observation to correspond with other committees and with the Council. They were vested with the power to arrest and examine suspected persons and if deemed necessary to hold them for trial by a higher tribunal. Members of the committees were to be elected annually by the freeholders.

Above these local committees was placed a system of district committees, one in each of the military districts, composed of a president and twelve members. The members were to be elected by the delegates in Congress from the counties which composed the several districts. They were to sit at least once in every three months. Power was given to them, subject to the authority of the Provincial Council, to direct the movements of the militia and other troops within their districts. They were to sit as courts for the trial of civil causes, for investigations into charges of disaffection to the American cause, and as appellate courts over the town and county committees. They shared with the Council authority to compel debtors suspected of intention to leave the province to give security to their creditors. Finally, they were to superintend the collection of the public revenue.

The Provincial Council was the chief executive authority of the new government. It was to be composed of thirteen members, one elected by the Congress for the province at large, and two from each of the military districts. Vacancies occurring during the recess of Congress were to be filled by the committee of safety for the district in which the vacancy fell. Military officers, except officers of the militia, were ineligible for membership. The members were to qualify by subscribing the oath prescribed for members of Congress. The Council was to meet once every three months, and a majority of the members was to constitute a quorum. Authority was given to them to direct the military operations of the province, to call out the militia when needed, and to execute the acts of the Assembly that were still in force with respect to the militia. They could issue commissions, suspend officers, order courts-martial, reject officers of the militia chosen by the people, and fill vacancies. But their real power lay in a sort of "general welfare" clause which empowered them "to do and transact all such matters and things as they may judge expedient to strengthen, secure and defend the colony." To carry out their powers, they were authorized to draw on the public treasury for such sums of money as they needed, for which they were accountable to Congress. In all matters they were given an appellate jurisdiction over the district committees, and in turn were subject to the authority of Congress. Their authority continued only during the recess of Congress, and Congress at each session was to review and pass upon their proceedings.

Such was the government that was to organize, equip and direct the military forces raised by Congress and to inaugurate the great war about to burst over the colony. As Saunders says, the die was now cast and North Carolina was at last a self-governing commonwealth. The people had so declared through representatives whom they had chosen after a campaign of forty days. Nobody was taken by surprise for all knew that the Congress elected in that campaign would formulate a provisional government. This action was taken fully eight months before the Continental Congress advised the colonies to adopt new constitutions. "The more the action of this great Hillsborough Congress is studied, and the events immediately preceding," writes Saunders, "the more wonderful seems the deliberate, well-considered, resolute boldness of our ancestors." [1]

The efficiency of the new government depended, of course, upon the men chosen to administer it. The members of the Provincial Council

---

[1] Col. Rec., Prefatory Notes, X, viii—ix.

were elected Sunday, September 10th. Samuel Johnston was chosen by the Congress for the province at large. The other members were: Cornelius Harnett and Samuel Ashe, for the Wilmington District; Thomas Jones and Whitmill Hill, for the Edenton District; Abner Nash and James Coor, for the New Bern District; Thomas Person and John Kinchen, for the Hillsboro District; Willie Jones and Thomas Eaton, for the Halifax District; Samuel Spencer and Waightstill Avery, for the Salisbury District.

On October 18th, the Council held its first session at Johnston Court House. "Among its members," says Bancroft,[1] "were Samuel Johnston; Samuel Ashe, a man whose integrity even his enemies never questioned, whose name a mountain county and the fairest town in the western part of the commonwealth keep in memory; Abner Nash, an eminent lawyer, described by Martin as 'the oracle of the committee of New Bern, and a principal supporter of sedition'; but on neither [sic] of these three did the choice of president fall: that office of peril and power was bestowed unanimously on Cornelius Harnett, of New Hanover, whose earnestness of purpose, and disinterested, unquenchable zeal had made him honored as the Samuel Adams of North Carolina. Thus prepared, the people of that colony looked toward the future with dignity and fearlessness."

[1] History of the United States, Ed, 1860, IV, 98.

Cornelius Harnett thus became the first chief executive of North Carolina independent of the Crown. Governor in all but name, he exercised greater authority than the people have since conferred on their chief executive, and occupied a position of honor and power, but likewise of responsibility and peril. "The office of president of the Council," as Jones observes,[1] "was the most arduous and dangerous post to which a citizen could be called, and, representing the executive officer of government, was exposed to all the abuse and insolence of the proclamations of the British authorities. The great energy of his [Harnett's] character, however, supported him through the difficulties of his station, and gave him the confidence and love of his countrymen." How he met the duties of his place may be read not only in the records of the Council, but also in the dispatches of the baffled and humiliated royal governor.

The Council were forced to work under the most unfavorable conditions. To begin with there was not a place in the province, except possibly the Palace at New Bern, suitable for their sessions. From necessity, as well as from policy, they became a migratory body. The members were subjected to almost every personal inconvenience and discomfort.[2] But these were among the least of their difficulties. Almost

---

[1] Defense of North Carolina, 206—207.

[2] MS. letter of Samuel Johnston, in the library of "Hayes"; copy in he collections of the North Carolina Historical Commission.

without any of the means with which governments usually administer public affairs, they
were compelled to struggle against political and
economic conditions that might well have daunted
the most determined. They had to rely for
success on a public sentiment which they themselves, to a large extent, had to create, and at
the same time to enforce measures that were
at once burdensome and dangerous. They had
no powerful press to uphold their hands. The
people were scattered over an immense area,
with means of communication crudely primitive.
There were no public highways except a few
rough and dangerous forest paths frequently
impassable. Their principal river was held at the
mouth by hostile ships of war, and at the head of
navigation by an enemy bold, hardy and enthu-
siastic in the king's cause. The East was domi-
nated by an oligarchy of wealthy planters and
merchants, living in an almost feudal state,
supported by slave labor; the West was a pure
democracy, composed of small farmers, living
on isolated farms, tilled by their own hands.
Both East and West, aristocracy and democracy,
were equally determined in their opposition to
the British government, but between the two,
right through the heart of the province, were
projected the Scotch Highlanders and the old
Regulators,—the one eager to prove their
loyalty to the throne against which they were

8

but recently in rebellion, the other equally as
eager to wreak vengeance upon the men who had
but lately crushed and humiliated them at Alamance. The province was a rural community
without a single center of population. There
were no mills or factories. Their only port
of any consequence was in the hands of the
enemy. Thus the Council's task was to organize
an army among a people divided in sentiment
and unused to war; to equip it without factories
for the manufacture of clothes, arms or ammunition; to train it without officers of experience;
to maintain it without money; and to direct
its movements in the face of an enemy superior
in numbers, in equipment, and in military experience.

The Council was created as a war measure,
and its principal work related to military affairs.[1]
The province was threatened in front and in the
rear. In front Governor Martin was organizing the Highlanders and Regulators for a
descent on the lower Cape Fear, and Governor
Dunmore, of Virginia, was encouraging an
insurrection of slaves on the Albemarle. In the
rear bands of Tories were overrunning western
South Carolina and threatening the frontier of
North Carolina, while the Indians, instigated
by British agents, were showing signs of restlessness. Foreseeing that the province would

---

[1] The proceedings of the Provincial Council are printed in the Colonial Records, X, 283—294, 349—362, 469—477.

"soon be invaded by British troops," the Council issued orders to Colonels Moore and Howe, of the continental regiments, to resist "to the utmost of their power" any attempt to invade the province; directed the committees of Wilmington and Brunswick to stop all communications, "on any pretense whatever," between the people and the governor, and "to cut off all supplies of provisions to any of the ships of war lying in Cape Fear River"; and commanded Colonels Griffith Rutherford and Thomas Polk, of the Salisbury District, to raise two regiments for defense of the frontier. Had they been less than tragical, these high-sounding orders, in comparison with the Council's means for enforcing them, would have been ludicrous. The Council found their minute-men and continental troops practically without clothes, arms, ammunition, or any of the necessary equipment of war, the people "destitute of sufficient arms for defense of their lives and property," and the outlook for supplying them unpromising enough. They drew upon every conceivable source. They bought and borrowed, made and mended, begged and confiscated, and though their efforts fell far short of what the emergency required, yet they were sufficient to enable the western militia to march to the aid of South Carolina on the famous "Snow Campaign;" to enable Colonel Howe to drive Lord Dunmore out of Norfolk;

and to enable Colonel Moore to win a brilliant campaign against the Highlanders at Moore's Creek Bridge. South Carolina and Virginia were profuse in their thanks to President Harnett for the important assistance in their hour of need,[1] while Governor Martin expressed great "mortification," and declared it was a matter "greatly to be lamented."

The defeat of the Highlanders at Moore's Creek Bridge, February 27th, 1776, was an event of much greater significance than is generally accorded to it in the histories of the Revolution; and Frothingham is guilty of no exaggeration when he calls it "the Lexington and Concord" of the South. So far from being an isolated event, it was part of an extensive campaign planned by the king and ministry for the subjugation of the southern colonies, which but for the victory at Moore's Creek Bridge would probably have succeeded. The plan was conceived by Governor Martin and heartily approved by the king. In brief, it was this. Martin was to organize the Highlanders and Regulators and march them to Wilmington. There they were to be joined by Lord Cornwallis with seven regiments of British regulars, escorted by a powerful fleet under Sir Peter Parker. Sir Henry Clinton with a force from the Boston army was to sail for the Cape Fear and take command. It was expected that North Carolina would

---

[1] State Records, XI, 267, 270, 274—75.

fall an easy victim to such a force, and then could be used as a basis of operations against Virginia, South Carolina and Georgia. The middle of February was the time set for the conjunction of the forces in the Cape Fear. Accordingly on February 18th, 1,600 Highlanders under the command of Donald McDonald, a veteran of Culloden and Bunker Hill, marched out of Cross Creek [1] and took the road for Wilmington. In the meantime the Whigs were concentrating their forces to oppose the march. Colonel James Moore was in chief command, and to him, more than to any other, the victory was due. Though not present in person at the battle, he directed the campaign which, on the morning of February 27th, brought Colonel Richard Caswell, with 1,100 militia, face to face with McDonald's 1,600 Highlanders at Moore's Creek Bridge, eighteen miles above Wilmington. The battle began about an hour before daybreak and lasted but a few minutes. The victory could not have been more decisive. The Whigs lost one man killed and one wounded. The total loss of the Highlanders was estimated at seventy. Their army was completely scattered. The victors captured 350 guns, 150 swords and dirks, 1,500 excellent rifles, a box containing £15,000 sterling, thirteen wagons, 850 soldiers and many officers including the commanding general. Two days after the victory Colonel Caswell reported

---

[1] Now Fayetteville.

it to President Harnett, and on March 2d, Colonel Moore sent to him a more detailed account of the campaign. [1]

The victory at Moore's Creek Bridge was the crowning achievement of the Provincial Council. But for the sleepless vigilance and resourceful energy of President Harnett and his colleagues in organizing, arming and equipping the troops, McDonald's march down the Cape Fear would have been but a holiday excursion. As it was, Governor Martin again measured strength with the people, and again was beaten. Clinton and Cornwallis came with their powerful armaments, but finding no loyalist force to welcome them at Cape Fear, they sailed away to beat in vain at the doors of Charleston. The victory at Moore's Creek Bridge saved North Carolina from conquest, and in all probability postponed the conquest of Georgia and South Carolina for three more years. Of this victory Bancroft writes:[2] "In less than a fortnight, more than nine thousand four hundred men of North Carolina rose against the enemy; and the coming of Clinton inspired no terror. * * * Almost every man was ready to turn out at an hour's warning. * * * Virginia offered assistance, and South Carolina would gladly have contributed relief; but North Carolina had men enough of her own to crush insurrection and guard against invasion; and

---

[1] Col. Rec., X, 482, 485 ; State Rec., XI, 383.

[2] History of the United States, ed. 1860, VIII, 289—90.

as they marched in triumph through their piney forests, they were persuaded that in their own woods they could win an easy victory over British regulars.   The terrors of a fate like that of Norfolk could not dismay the patriots of Wilmington; the people spoke more and more of independence; and the Provincial Congress, at its impending session, was expected to give an authoritative form to the prevailing desire."

VIII

INDEPENDENCE

"Moore's Creek was the Rubicon over which North Carolina passed to independence and constitutional self-government." Before that event the Whig leaders had rather dreaded than sought independence. They met with indignant denial the assertions of their enemies that they had aimed at it from the beginning of their dispute with the mother country. Perhaps they did not foresee as clearly as the Tories did the logical result of their contentions. At any rate, they approached independence slowly, through a long process of development, and finally adopted it, as emancipation was afterwards adopted, as a war measure. Officially North Carolina led the way, and Cornelius Harnett wrote the first resolution adopted by any of the colonies authorizing their delegates in the Continental Congress to vote for independence. It seems proper, therefore, to trace briefly the rise and development of the sentiment for independence in North Carolina, and to point out what influence the action of the North Carolina Congress had in other colonies.

It can not be said that the sentiment for independence "originated" in any particular place. It was a growth and was present, perhaps unconsciously, in the minds of political philosophers for some time before England's conduct crystallized it into conscious thought. Academic discussions of the possibility of an independent American nation were not uncommon, either in Europe or America, for many years before the Revolution; but it is safe to say that the idea took no definite shape even in the minds of the most advanced thinkers until after the struggle over the Stamp Act. The principles upon which the Americans opposed the Stamp Act had been regarded in the colonies as so firmly fixed, both by the British Constitution and by the colonial charters, that they were astonished to find them seriously questioned. Adherence to their charters and resistance to their perversion were cardinal principles with North Carolinians throughout their colonial history, and their records for a hundred years before the passage of the Stamp Act are full of assertions of the principles upon which the American Revolution was fought.

The ministry therefore no sooner asserted the constitutional authority of Parliament to levy taxes on the colonists, than the people of North Carolina denied it. Their contest, however, before the outbreak of hostilities was for constitutional government within the British Empire, though a few far-sighted leaders soon began to think of independence as possibly the ultimate solution of their political troubles with the mother country. Among the leaders of North Carolina who foresaw it, first place must be assigned to William Hooper. On April 26, 1774, in a letter to James Iredell, Hooper made this remarkable forecast of the political tendencies of the time:

"With you I anticipate the important share which the colonies must soon have in regulating the political balance. They are striding fast to independence, and ere long will build an empire upon the ruins of Great Britain, will adopt its constitution purged of its impurities, and from an experience of its defects will guard against those evils which have wasted its vigor and brought it to an untimely end." [1]

In the same prophetic vein Samuel Johnston a few months later, September 23, referring more specifically than Hooper to the quarrel with the mother country, wrote to a friend in London:

"The ministry from the time of passing the Declaratory Act, on the repeal of the Stamp Act, seem to have used every opportunity of teasing and fretting the people here as if on purpose to draw them into rebellion or some violent opposition to government; at a time when the inhabitants of Boston were, every man, quietly employed about their own private affairs, the wise members of your House of Commons on the authority of ministerial scribbles, declare they are in a state of open rebellion. On the

---

[1] Col. Rec., IX, 983—86.

strength of this they pass a set of laws which from their severity and injustice can not be carried into execution but by a military force, which they have very wisely provided, being conscious that no people who had once tasted the sweets of freedom would ever submit to them except in the last extremity. They have now brought things to a crisis and God only knows where it will end. It is useless in disputes between different countries to talk about the right which one has to give laws to the other, as that generally attends the power, though where that power is wantonly or cruelly exercised there are instances where the weaker state has resisted with success; for when once the sword is drawn, all nice distinctions fall to the ground; the difference between internal and external taxation will be little attended to, and it will hereafter be considered of no consequence whether the act be to regulate trade or raise a fund to support a majority in the House of Commons. By this desperate push the ministry will either confirm their power of making laws to bind the colonies in all cases whatsoever, or give up the right of making laws to bind them in any case." [1]

Johnston's letter is more to the point than Hooper's; for while Hooper wrote in a speculative academic vein, basing his conclusions upon a fancied analogy between the Roman Empire

---

[1] Col. Rec., IX, 1071—72.

in its decline and the British Empire, Johnston was discussing the specific issues in dispute between the two countries, and, as events subsequently showed, correctly pointed out their logical result. He regarded the dispute as one "between different countries," and looked to separation and revolution for the salvation of the weaker.

These utterances, however, expressed political judgment rather than sentiment, for neither Hooper nor Johnston at that time desired independence. Nor did their judgment express the general sentiment of the colony. This sentiment found more accurate expression in the proceedings of the local meetings which were held in the various counties during the summer of 1774 to elect delegates to the Provincial Congress, and to adopt instructions to them. These instructions invariably required the delegates to take a firm stand for the constitutional rights of the colonists, but at the same time most of them professed the utmost loyalty to the king. Rowan county, for instance, August 8, instructed its delegates to make a declaration that the people of Rowan were ready at any time to defend with their lives and fortunes "his Majesty's right and title to the Crown of Great Britain and his Dominions in America;"[1] while Johnston county, four days later, declared "that his Majesty's subjects in North America owe the

---

[1] Col. Rec., IX, 1024.

same allegiance to the Crown of Great Britain that is due from his subjects born in that kingdom or elsewhere."[1] But both meetings were equally emphatic in claiming for the king's subjects in America "the same rights and liberties that his subjects within the Kingdom of Great Britain" enjoyed; hence they regarded taxation by Parli ment as unjust, oppressive and unconstitutional, and thought it ought to be resisted. These professions of loyalty and claims to immunity from taxation by Parliament, are typical of the sentiment prevailing in the local meetings, and it is not necessary to quote others.[2] Besides, the Provincial Congress, August 27, spoke for the province as a whole when it resolved "to maintain and defend the succession of the House of Hanover as by law established," and avowed "inviolable and unshaken fidelity" to George III.[3]

While these expressions undoubtedly represent the general sentiment of the colony at that time, they are less significant than other utterances which point to the change unconsciously working in the minds of men. The first Provincial Congress, for instance, was the result of John Harvey's demand for "a convention independent of the governor;"[4] and the general meeting at Wilmington, July 21, which issued the call for a congress, emphasized the "constitutional liber-

[1] Col. Rec., IX, 1031.
[2] Col. Rec., IX, 1037, 1038, 1104.
[3] Col. Rec., IX, 1044.
[4] Col. Rec., IX, 968.

ties of America," but neglected to make any mention of allegiance or loyalty to the king.[1] Anson county, August 18, also omitted a profession of loyalty to the Crown though denouncing in vigorous language "the late arbitrary and cruel acts of the British Parliament and other unconstitutional and oppressive measures of the British Ministry."[2] More significant than either were the instructions of Pitt county. Pitt's delegates were instructed to make "a declaration of American rights," and, while acknowledging "due subjection to the Crown of England," to make it equally clear that in submitting to the authority of the king, the Americans did so "by their own voluntary act," and were entitled to enjoy "all their free chartered rights and liberties as British free subjects."[3] But surpassing all other resolutions in the clearness and accuracy with which they stated the American idea, and reaching the most advanced ground attained in North Carolina during the year 1774, were the instructions of Granville county, adopted August 15. They declared "that those absolute rights we are entitled to as men, by the immutable laws of nature, are antecedent to all social and relative duties whatsoever; that by the civil compact subsisting between our king and his people, allegiance is the right of the first

---

1 Col. Rec., IX, 1016.
2 Col. Rec., IX, 1022.
3 Col. Rec., IX, 1030.

magistrate, and protection the right of the people; that a violation of this compact would rescind the civil institution binding both king and people together." [1]

Political sentiment in North Carolina, therefore, during the year 1774 reached this point: The people owe and acknowledge allegiance to the king, but in return for this allegiance the king owes protection to the people; if either violates the "civil compact" subsisting between them, the other is released from all obligations to maintain it; however, the acts of which the people now complain are not the acts of the king, but of a corrupt Parliament and a venal and tyrannical ministry; the people are convinced that the king, if only they could reach the royal ears with their grievances, would throw the mantle of his protection around them; and therefore they determined, in the words of the Granville resolutions: "Although we are oppressed, we will still adhere to the civil obligation exacting our allegiance to the best of kings, as we entertain a most cordial affection to his Majesty's person."

A severe blow was dealt this position with the opening of the year 1775. In February the two houses of Parliament presented an address to the king declaring the colonies in rebellion, and assuring his Majesty of their determination to support him in his efforts to suppress it; and the king returning his thanks for their loyal

---

[1] Col. Rec., IX, 1034.

address, called for an increase of both the land
and naval forces to be used in America. A few
months later those who held that the king was
not responsible for the acts of Parliament were
still further shaken in their position by the
announcement that he was hiring Hessians for
service against the Americans; and in October
they were driven completely from their ground
by his proclamation declaring the colonists out
of his protection.

The effect of these measures on the development of sentiment for independence is marked,
first in the opinion of individual leaders, afterwards in the utterances of public assemblies.
On April 7, just after the adjournment of the
second Provincial Congress and the dissolution
of the last Assembly held under royal authority,
Governor Martin, in a letter to Lord Dartmouth,
assured his lordship that he had taken every
measure n his power "to resist the growth of a
most daring spirit of sedition and disorder that
is gaining ground here very fast. * * * I am
bound in conscience and duty to add, my Lord,"
he continued, "that government is here as absolutely prostrate as impotent, and that nothing
but the shadow of it is left. * * * I must
further say, too, my Lord, that it is my serious
opinion, which I communicate with the last
degree of concern, that unless effectual measures
such as British spirit may dictate are speedily

taken there will not long remain a trace of Britain's dominion over these colonies."[1] Three months later Joseph Hewes considered himself "over head and ears in what the ministry call rebellion," but felt "no compunction" for the part he had taken, or for the number of "enemies lately slain in the battle at Bunker's Hill."[2] Another North Carolina Whig writing, July 31, to a business house in Edinburgh, declared that "every American, to a man, is determined to die or be free," and though professing loyalty to the king and disclaiming a desire for independence he closed his letter with the warning: "This country, without some step is taken, and that soon, will be inevitably lost to the mother country."[3] Thomas McKnight, a Tory, believed there had been "from the beginning of the dispute a fixed design in some people's breasts to throw off every connection with Great Britain and to act for the future as totally independent."[4] After the king's proclamation in October, Hewes at Philadelphia entertained "but little expectation of a reconciliation" and saw "scarcely a dawn of hope that it will take place";[5] and thought that independence would come soon "if the British ministry pursue their present diabolical scheme."[6]

---

[1] Col. Rec., IX, 1214—15.

[2] Col. Rec., X, 86.

[3] Col. Rec., X, 123.

[4] Col. Rec., X, 249.

[5] Col. Rec., X, 315.

[6] Hazelton : The Declaration of Independence ; Its History, 31.

9

The year 1775 closed in North Carolina with the publication of a remarkable open letter addressed to "The Inhabitants of the United Colonies," and signed by one who called himself "A British American." He reviewed the causes of the dispute with the mother country; declared that the colonies had been forced against their wishes into a "just, necessary and honourably defensive war;" and maintained that

"There is yet a way open for us, not only to escape the threatened ruin, but to become a happy, wealthy, powerful and respectable people. If it be asked how this great work is to be effected, I answer:

"First. By declaring an immediate independency;

"Secondly. By holding forth, to all the Powers of Europe, a general neutrality;

"Thirdly. By immediately opening all our ports, and declaring them free to every European Power, except Great Britain, and inviting foreigners to purchase our commodities, and to furnish us with arms, ammunition, and such manufactures as we can not, as yet, furnish ourselves with; which we can not do with any prospect of success, so long as we retain even but the shadow of dependence on, or subjection to Great Britain. * * *

"We must separate, or become the laboring slaves of Britain, which we disdain to be. * *

These things, I hope, will be duly considered by every inhabitant of America, as they are recommended to them to show the absurdity of continuing to petition and address, while our towns are in flames, and our inhabitants murdered, rather than separate from a cruel, bloodthirsty people, the cause of all our woes."[1]

Men of course are more radical in expressing their opinions in private than in public assemblies and official documents. It will be found, therefore, that during the year 1775 the sentiment of public assemblies, though much in advance of the sentiment of 1774, was more conservatively expressed than the private opinions of the leaders might lead us to expect. On April 6, 1775, the Assembly of the province, in reply to a message from the governor reminding them of their duty to the king, declared that "the Assembly of North Carolina have the highest sense of the allegiance due to the king; the oath so repeatedly taken by them to that purpose made it unnecessary for them to be reminded of it"; at the same time, however, they called the governor's attention to the fact that the king "was by the same constitution that established that allegiance and enjoined that oath, happily for his subjects, solemnly bound to protect them in all their just rights and privileges by which a reciprocal duty became incumbent upon both."[2]

---

[1] Force's American Archives, 4th Series, IV, 470—73.
[2] Col. Rec., IX, 1198.

This declaration was made before the people
had heard of the address of Parliament in February and the king's reply declaring them in rebellion. How quickly they assumed that the
withdrawal of protection by the sovereign
released the subject from the obligations of
allegiance is made manifest by the Mecklenburg
Resolutions of May 31. "Whereas," so runs
this striking document, "by an address presented
to his Majesty by both houses of Parliament in
February last, the American colonies are declared
to be in a state of actual rebellion, we conceive
that all laws and commissions confirmed by or
derived from the authority of the king and Parliament are annulled and vacated and the former
civil constitution of these colonies for the present
wholly suspended;" therefore, it was resolved
that "the Provincial Congress of each province
under the direction of the great Continental
Congress is invested with all legislative and
executive powers within their respective provinces
and that no other legislative or executive power
does or can exist at this time in any of these
colonies." Under these circumstances it was
thought necessary to inaugurate a new county
government, to organize the militia, and to
elect officials "who shall hold and exercise their
several powers by virtue of this choice and
independent of the Crown of Great Britain and
former constitution of this province." These

resolves and this organization were declared to be "in full force and virtue until instructions from the Provincial Congress regulating the jurisprudence of the province shall provide otherwise or the legislative body of Great Britain resign its unjust and arbitrary pretensions with respect to America." [1]

The day after the meeting at Charlotte, the Rowan committee, which had declared a year before that they were ready to die in defense of the king's title to his American dominions, resolved, "that by the constitution of our government we are a free people"; that the constitution "limits both sovereignty and allegiance," and "that it is our duty to surrender our lives before our constitutional privileges to any set of men upon earth." [2] And, finally, in August, just before the meeting of the Provincial Congress, Tryon county resolved to bear true allegiance to the king, but only "so long as he secures to us those rights and liberties which the principles of our constitution require. " [3]

Thus it seems clear that when the Provincial Congress met in August, 1775, the entire province had reached the advanced ground on which Granville county stood in August of 1774. But just as these local assemblies were more conservative in expressing their sentiments than

---

[1] Col. Rec., IX, 1282—84.

[2] Col. Rec., X, 10—11.

[3] Col. Rec., X, 163. See also IX, 1149, 1160—64 ; X, 26, 29, 61, 171, and 239.

individuals, so the Provincial Congress was more conservative than the local assemblies, though both were controlled largely by the same men. This Congress, September 8, unanimously adopted an address to "The Inhabitants of the British Empire," in which they said:

"To enjoy the fruits of our own honest industry, to call that our own which we earn with the labor of our hands and the sweat of our brows; to regulate that internal policy by which we and not they [Parliament] are to be affected; these are the mighty boons we ask. And traitors, rebels, and every harsh appellation that malice can dictate or the virulence of language express, are the returns which we receive to the most humble petitions and earnest supplications. We have been told that independence is our object; that we seek to shake off all connection with the parent state. Cruel suggestion! Do not all our professions, all our actions, uniformly contradict this?

"We again declare, and we invoke that Almighty Being who searches the recesses of the human heart and knows our most secret intentions, that it is our most earnest wish and prayer to be restored with the other United Colonies to the state in which we and they were placed before the year 1763. * * *

"Whenever we have departed from the forms of the constitution, our own safety and self-preservation have dictated the expedient; and if in any instances we have assumed powers which the laws invest in the sovereign or his representatives, it has been only in defense of our persons, properties and those rights which God and the constitution have made unalienably ours. As soon as the cause of our fears and apprehensions are removed, with joy will we return these powers to their regular channels; and such institutions formed from mere necessity, shall end with that necessity that created them.'"[1]

Soon after the adjournment of this Congress came news of the king's proclamation in October declaring the Americans out of his protection and commanding his armies and navy to levy war against them. After this nothing more is heard from public assemblies and conventions of loyalty to the Crown. Sentiment hastened rapidly toward independence. "My first wish is to be free," declared Hooper, a delegate in the Continental Congress; "my second to be reconciled to Great Britain."[2] Six days later, February 12, 1776, John Penn, also a delegate in the Continental Congress, wrote to his friend Thomas Person:

"I learn that Governor Martin has at length obtained his wishes; administration having agreed to send seven regiments to North Caro-

---

[1] Col. Rec., X, 201.

[2] Alderman : William Hooper, 40.

lina. * * * I make no doubt but the Southern Provinces will soon be the scene of action. * * I hope we to the Southward shall act like men determined to be free. * * * Should they [Parliament and the ministry] persevere in their attempts to reduce us to a state of slavery by carrying on this unnatural war with fire and sword, we must determine to act with unanimity and assume every power of government for the purpose of legislation in order to be the better able to defend ourselves. * * * For God's sake, my good sir, encourage our people, animate them to dare even to die for their country." [1]

Two days later he took an even more advanced position.

"Our dispute with Britain," he wrote, "grows serious indeed. Matters are drawing to a crisis. They seem determined to persevere and are forming alliances against us. Must we not do something of the like nature? Can we hope to carry on a war without having trade or commerce somewhere? Can we ever pay any taxes without it? Will not our paper money depreciate if we go on emitting? These are serious things and require your consideration. The consequence of making alliances is perhaps a total separation with Britain and without something of that sort we may not be able to provide what is necessary for our defense." [2]

[1] Col. Rec., X, 449.
[2] Col. Rec., X, 456.

And Hewes, writing from Congress to Samuel Johnston, March 20, declared:

"I see no prospect of a reconciliation. Nothing is left now but to fight it out. * * * Some among us urge strongly for independency and eternal separation; others wish to wait a little longer and to have the opinion of their constituents on that subject. You must give us the sentiment of your province when your convention meets." [1]

Thus spoke the three delegates in the Continental Congress; but in no respect were they in advance of their constituents. Samuel Johnston, writing March 3, expressed the opinion that the future might "offer a more favorable crisis for throwing off our connection with Great Britain;" but added:

"It is, however, highly probable from anything that I have yet been able to learn of the disposition of the people at home, from the public papers, for I have not lately received any letters, that the colonies will be under the necessity of throwing off their allegiance to the king and Parliament of Great Britain this summer. If France and Spain are hearty and sincere in our cause, or sufficiently apprised of the importance of the connection with us to risk war with Great Britain, we shall undoubtedly succeed; if they are irresolute and play a doubtful game I shall not think our success so certain." [2]

---

[1] State Records of North Carolina, XI, 288—9.

[2] MS. letter in the library at "Hayes." Copy in the collections of he North Carolina Historical Commission.

Replying to Hewes's inquiry of March 20th, he said:

"I am inclined to think with you that there is little prospect of an accommodation. You wish to know my sentiments on the subjects of treating with foreign powers and the independence of the Colonies. I have apprehensions that no foreign power will treat with us till we disclaim our dependence on Great Britain and I would wish to have assurances that they would afford us effectual service before we take that step. I have, I assure you, no other scruples on this head; the repeated insults and injuries we have received from the people of my native island has [sic] done away all my partiality for a connection with them and I have no apprehensions of our being able to establish and support an independence if France and Spain would join us cordially and risque a war with Great Britain in exchange for our trade." [1]

In a letter written from Petersburg, Virginia, April 12th, the writer says:

"From several letters I have received from North Carolina since that convention met, I find they are for independence, as they either have, or intend to repeal the instructions that were given to their delegates, and to leave them at liberty to vote, upon every occasion, as they may think best. Mr.—— was some little time

---

[1] MS. letter in the library at "Hayes." Copy in the collections of the North Carolina Historical Commission.

at Halifax. He says they are quite spirited
and unanimous; indeed, I hear nothing praised
but 'Common Sense' and Independence. The people of North Carolina are making great preparations, and say they are determined to die hard."[1]

On April 14, Hooper and Penn arrived at
Halifax from Philadelphia. Three days later
Hooper wrote to Hewes, who had remained at
Philadelphia, and Penn wrote to John Adams,
describing the situation as they found it in Vir-
ginia and North Carolina.

"My progress through Virginia," said Hooper,
"was marked with nothing extraordinary.
* * * The language of Virginia is uni
formly for independence. If there is a single
man in that province who preaches a different
doctrine I had not the fortune to fall in his
company. But rapid as the change has been in
Virginia, North Carolina has the honour of going
far before them. Our late instructions afford
you some specimen of the temper of the present
Congress and of the people at large. It would
be more than unpopular, it would be Toryism,
to hint the possibility of future reconciliation.
For my part if it were my sentiment that such
conduct was premature, I should not think it
prudent to avow it. We can not stem a torrent
and one had better swim on the democratic flood
than, vainly attempting to check it, be buried
in it. * * * Britain has lost us by a series

---

[1] Force's American Archives, 4th Series, V, 862.

of impolitic, wicked and savage actions as would
have disgraced a nation of Hottentots. Human
patience can bear no more and all ranks of
people cry, 'that the cup of bitterness is full and
running over. Let the miseries of *separation*
be what they will they can not enhance our
misery. We may be better, we can not be worse.'
Thus they reason and when I survey what has
been done I have too much the feeling of a man
to attempt to reason them out of this effusion."[1]

Likewise wrote Penn:

"As I came through Virginia I found the
inhabitants desirous to be independent from
Britain. However, they were willing to submit their opinion on the subject to whatever the General Congress should determine.
North Carolina by far exceeds them occasioned
by the great fatigue, trouble and danger the
people here have undergone for some time past.
Gentlemen of the first fortune in the province
have marched as common soldiers; and to
encourage and give spirit to the men have footed
it the whole time. Lord Cornwallis with seven
regiments is expected to visit us every day.
Clinton is now in Cape Fear with Governor
Martin, who has about forty sail of vessels,
armed and unarmed, waiting his arrival. The
Highlanders and Regulators are not to be trusted.
Governor Martin has coaxed a number of slaves

[1] MS. letter in the library at "Hayes." Copy in the collections of
the North Carolina Historical Commission.

to leave their masters in the lower parts; everything base and wicked is practiced by him. These things have wholly changed the temper and disposition of the inhabitants that are friends to liberty; all regard or fondness for the king or nation of Britain is gone; a total separation is what they want. Independence is the word most used. They ask if it is possible that any colony after what has passed can wish for a reconciliation? The convention have tried to get the opinion of the people at large. I am told that in many counties there was not one dissenting voice." [1]

Thus in letters, in conversations by the fireside and at the cross-roads, in newspapers, and in public assemblies, the Whig leaders worked steadily to mould public sentiment in favor of a Declaration of Independence. But the crowning arguments that converted thousands to this view were the guns of Caswell and Lillington at Moore's Creek Bridge in the early morning hours of February 27, and the black hulks of Sir Henry Clinton's men-of-war as they rode at anchor below Brunswick. Moore's Creek Bridge, says Frothingham, "was the Lexington and Concord of that region. The newspapers circulated the details of this brilliant result. The spirits of the Whigs ran high. 'You never,'

---

[1] Quoted by Swain in "The British Invasion in 1776," published in Cooke's "Revolutionary History of North Carolina," 125. There incorrectly dated as April 7, 1776. See Hazelton's "Declaration of Independence," 83, 402.

one wrote, 'knew the like in your life for true
patriotism.'"[1]   In the midst of this excitement
the Provincial Congress met, April 4, at Halifax.
The next day Samuel Johnston wrote: "All our
people here are up for independence,"[2]   and
added a few days later: "We are going to the
devil * * * without knowing how to help
ourselves, and though many are sensible of this,
yet they would rather go that way than to
submit to the British ministry. * * * Our
people are full of the idea of independence."[3]
"Independence seems to be the word," wrote
General Robert Howe; "I know not one dissenting voice."[4]

To this position, then, within a year, the
king had driven his faithful subjects of North
Carolina and they now expected their Congress
to give formal and public expression to their
sentiments. When Hooper and Penn arrived
at Halifax they found that the Congress had
already spoken. On April 8, six days before
their arrival, a committee was appointed, composed of Cornelius Harnett, Allen Jones, Thomas
Burke, Abner Nash, John Kinchen, Thomas
Person, and Thomas Jones, "to take into consideration the usurpations and violences attempted and committed by the king and Parliament

---

[1] The Rise of the Republic, 503.

[2] McRee's Life and Correspondence of James Iredell, I, 275.

[3] MS. letter in library at "Hayes."   Copy in the collections of the
North Carolina Historical Commission.

[4] Hazelton: Declaration of Independence, 84.

of Britain against America, and the further measures to be taken for frustrating the same, and for the better defense of this province." [1] To Cornelius Harnett fell the task of drafting the committee's report. With great self-control, in a report remarkable for its calm dignity and restraint, but alive with suppressed emotion, he drew an indictment against the British ministry not equaled by any similar document of the Revolutionary period, except only the great Declaration itself. After deliberating for four days, on April 12th, this committee, through Cornelius Harnett, submitted its report. "In ringing sentences, not unworthy of Burke or Pitt," says Dr. Smith, "the report set forth in a short preamble the usurpations of the British ministry and 'the moderation hitherto manifested by the United Colonies.' Then came the declaration which to those who made it meant long years of desolating war, smoking homesteads, widowed mothers, and fatherless children, but to us and our descendants a heritage of imperishable glory." [2] This is the report which Cornelius Harnett read and the Congress unanimously adopted:

"It appears to your committee, that pursuant to the plan concerted by the British ministry for subjugating America, the king and Parliament of Great Britain have usurped a power

---

[1] Col. Rec., X, 504.

[2] C. Alphonso Smith: Our Debt to Cornelius Harnett: North Carolina University Magazine, May, 1907, 392.

over the persons and properties of the people unlimited and uncontrolled; and disregarding their
humble petitions for peace, liberty and safety,
have made divers legislative acts, denouncing
war, famine, and every species of calamity,
against the continent in general. That British
fleets and armies have been, and still are daily
employed in destroying the people, and committing the most horrid devastations on the country.
That governors in different colonies have declared
protection to slaves who should imbrue their
hands in the blood of their masters. That ships
belonging to America are declared prizes of war,
and many of them have been violently seized
and confiscated. In consequence of all which
multitudes of the people have been destroyed, or
from easy circumstances reduced to the most
lamentable distress.

"And whereas the moderation hitherto manifested by the United Colonies and their sincere
desire to be reconciled to the mother country
on constitutional principles, have procured no
mitigation of the aforesaid wrongs and usurpations, and no hopes remain of obtaining redress
by those means alone which have been hitherto
tried, your committee are of opinion that the
House should enter into the following resolve,
to wit:

"Resolved, That the delegates for this colony in
the Continental Congress be impowered to con-

cur with the delegates of the other colonies in
declaring independency, and forming foreign
alliances, reserving to this colony the sole and
exclusive right of forming a constitution and
laws for this colony, and of appointing delegates
from time to time (under the direction of a
general representation thereof,) to meet the
delegates of the other colonies for such purposes
as shall be hereafter pointed out." [1]

"Thus," declares Frothingham, "the popular
party carried North Carolina as a unit in favor
of independence, when the colonies from New
England to Virginia were in solid array against
it." [2] Comment is unnecessary. The actors,
the place, the occasion, the time, the action
itself, tell their own story. "The American
Congress," declared Bancroft, "needed an impulse
from the resolute spirit of some colonial convention, and the example of a government springing
wholly from the people. * * * The word
which South Carolina hesitated to pronounce
was given by North Carolina. That colony,
proud of its victory over domestic enemies, and
roused to defiance by the presence of Clinton,
the British general, in one of their rivers, * *
unanimously" voted for separation. "North
Carolina was the first colony to vote explicit
sanction to independence." [3]

---

[1] Col. Rec., X, 512.

[2] The Rise of the Republic, p. 504.

[3] History of the United States, ed. 1860, VIII, 345—352. The language, but not the sense, is slightly modified in later editions.

10

A copy of the resolution was immediately hurried off to Joseph Hewes at Philadelphia.[1] Its effect on the movement for independence in the other colonies was felt at once. "This was a move of the greatest importance," says Elson, "and it was but a short time until Rhode Island and then Massachusetts followed the example of their Southern sister."[2] Frothingham declares: "The example was warmly welcomed by the patriots, and commended for imitation."[3] The correspondence of the period bears out his statement. The newspapers printed the resolution and held it up to the other colonies as an example to be followed. The leaders in the Continental Congress hastened to lay it before their constituents. Samuel Adams, the foremost man in New England in fostering the sentiment for independence, wrote, April 30, to a friend in Boston:

"The idea of independence spreads far and wide among the colonies. Many of the leading men see the absurdity of supposing that allegiance is due to a sovereign who has already thrown us out of his protection. * * * The convention of North Carolina has * * * revoked certain instructions which tied the hands of their delegates here. Virginia, whose convention is to meet on the 3d of next month, will follow the

---

[1] Col. Rec., X, 495, 604.

[2] History of the United States, 252.

[3] The Rise of the Republic, 504.

lead. * * * We can not make events; our business is wisely to improve them. * * * Mankind are governed more by their feelings than by reason. Events which excite those feelings will produce wonderful events. The Boston Port Bill suddenly wrought an union of the colonies which could not have been brought about by the industry of years in reasoning on the necessity of it for the common safety. * * * * The burning of Norfolk and the hostilities committed in North Carolina have kindled the resentment of our Southern brethren, who once thought their Eastern friends hotheaded and rash. Now, indeed, the tone is altered, and it is said that the coolness and moderation of the one is necessary to allay the heat of the other. There is reason that would induce one to wish for the speedy arrival of the British troops that are expected at the Southward. I think our friends are well prepared for them, and one battle would do more towards a Declaration of Independence than a long chain of conclusive arguments in a Provincial Convention or the Continental Congress." [1]

The next day, May 1, Elbridge Gerry, another of the delegates from Massachusetts in the Continental Congress, wrote with reference to independence:

"I am glad you approve the proposals for

[1] Wells: The Life and Public Services of Samuel Adams, Vol. 2, pp. 294—6.

instructions, and can with pleasure inform you that North Carolina has taken off from their [sic] delegates the restrictions relative to this matter, and as I am informed has left them at liberty to vote for a final separation from Great Britain." [1]

The 28th of the same month, after Virginia had followed the example of North Carolina, he wrote:

"Some days since I enclosed to our worthy friend Major Hawley sundry newspapers containing intelligence of importance, but not so agreeable in its nature as the enclosed papers announce relative to our sister colonies of Virginia and North Carolina. Their conventions have unanimously declared for independency, and have in this respect exceeded their sister colonies in a most noble and decisive measure. I hope it will be forthwith communicated to your honorable Assembly, and hope to see my native colony follow this laudable example." [2]

Three days later he recurred again to the same subject:

"The conviction which the late measures of administration have brought to the minds of doubting persons has such an effect, that I think the colonies can not long remain an independent depending people, but that they will declare

---

[1] Austin: The Life of Elbridge Gerry, p. 178.
[2] Ibid.: pp. 180–1.

themselves as their interest and safety have long required, entirely separated from the prostituted government of Great Britain * * * The principal object of our attention at this important time, I think, should be the manufacturing arms, lead and clothing, and obtaining flints, for I suppose since the measures adopted by North Carolina and Virginia that there can not remain a doubt with our Assembly of the propriety of declaring for independency, and therefore that our thoughts will be mostly directed to the means for supporting it." [1]

May 29 Cæsar Rodney, a delegate from Delaware, wrote to Thomas Rodney:

"The colonies of North Carolina and Virginia have both by their conventions declared for Independence by a unanimous vote; and have instructed their members to move and vote for it in Congress." [2]

Perhaps no man welcomed with greater joy the example of North Carolina in moving for independence than John Adams, the great "Colossus of Independence." Writing May 29 to a friend in regard to the British vessels in Boston harbor, he said:

"I am much pleased with your spirited project of driving away the wretches from the harbor, and never shall be happy till I hear it is done, and the very entrance fortified impregnably.

---

[1] Hazelton : The Declaration of Independence, p. 107.
[2] Ibid., 425.

I can not bear that an unfriendly flag should be in sight of Bacon [sic] Hill. You are 'checked by accounts from the southward, of a disposition in a great majority to counteract independence.' Read the proceedings of Georgia, South and North Carolina, and Virginia, and then judge."[1]

And again, June 1, he wrote to Isaac Smith:

"Your observations upon the oppressive severity of the old regulations of trade * * * are very just. But if you consider the resolution of Congress, and that of Virginia of the 15th of May, the resolutions of the two Carolinas and Georgia, each of which colonies are instituting new governments under the authority of the people, * * * I believe you will be convinced that there is little probability of our ever again coming under the yoke of British regulations of trade." [2]

Thus was the example of North Carolina welcomed by the advocates of independence who urged their constituents to follow her lead. Virginia did so May 15, and on the 27th of the same month, just after Joseph Hewes had presented to the Continental Congress the resolution of the North Carolina Congress, the delegates from Virginia presented their instructions. [3] Virginia had gone one step further than North Carolina, for while the latter "impowered" her

---

[1] C. F. Adams : The Works of John Adams, IX, 379.

[2] Ibid., IX, 383.

[3] Ford : Journals of the Continental Congress, IV, 397.

delegates to "concur" with the other colonies in declaring independence, the former "instructed" her representatives to "propose" it. Hence it was that Richard Henry Lee, of Virginia, and not Joseph Hewes, of North Carolina, won the distinction of moving "that these United Colonies are and of right ought to be free and independent States." Richard Henry Lee well deserves his great fame as a Revolutionary statesman, but it ought not to be forgotten that in the great act of moving for independence he trod the way which Cornelius Harnett had already marked out.

IX

THE INDEPENDENT GOVERNMENT

After the Resolution of April 12th, the Congress of North Carolina proceeded as if independence were an assured fact. Immediately the task of reorganizing the government was taken up. On April 13th a committee was appointed "to prepare a temporary civil constitution."[1] Prominent among the members of this committee were Johnston, Nash, Harnett, Burke, and Person. Hooper was afterwards added. They were men of political sagacity and ability, but their ideas of the kind of constitution that ought to be adopted were wofully inharmonious. Heretofore in the measures of resistance to the British ministry remarkable unanimity had prevailed in the councils of the Whigs. But when they undertook to frame a constitution faction at once raised its head. In after years historians designated these factions as "Conservatives" and "Radicals." These terms carry their own meaning, and need no further explanation, but perhaps it may not be out of place to say that while both were equally devoted to constitutional liberty, the Radicals seem to have laid the greater emphasis upon "liberty," the Conservatives upon the modifier "constitutional." Of the members of the committee, Thomas

---

[1] Col. Rec., X, 515.

Person was the leader of the former, Samuel Johnston of the latter. As the lines between the two factions were not sharply drawn, it is not always possible to assign prominent politicians to either; indeed, many of them would not have admitted that they belonged to any faction, for agreeing with some of the views of both, they agreed with the extreme views of neither. To this class Cornelius Harnett seems to have belonged. His contributions to the constitutional history of the State indicate that he was not so conservative as Johnston nor so radical as Person, while throughout his career he retained the respect and confidence of both.

Congress soon found that no agreement could be reached, while continued debate on the constitution would consume time that ought to be given to more urgent matters. Accordingly on April 30th, the committee was discharged and a second committee appointed to frame "a temporary form of government until the end of the next Congress." This committee brought in a report on May 11th, which the Congress promptly adopted.[1]   But few changes were made in the plan already in operation, but these changes were not without significance. The district committees of safety were abolished. The term "Provincial" was thought to be no longer appropriate and "Council of Safety" was accordingly substituted for "Provincial Council."

---

[1] Col. Rec., X, 579.

No change was made in its organization. The Provincial Council had been required to sit once in every three months; the Council of Safety was to sit continuously, and its authority was considerably extended. All the powers of its predecessor were bequeathed to it, while among its additional powers was the authority to grant letters of marque and reprisal; to establish courts and appoint judges of admiralty; and to appoint commissioners of navigation to enforce the trade regulations of the Continental and Provincial Congresses.

The election of the members of the Council of Safety revealed the growth of factions. Willie Jones, chief of the Radicals, defeated Samuel Johnston for member at large. Other changes in the membership were as follows: in the New Bern District, John Simpson for Abner Nash; in the Halifax District, Joseph John Williams in place of Willie Jones; in the Hillsboro District, John Rand for John Kinchen; in the Salisbury District, Hezekiah Alexander and William Sharpe, both new members. Two only of the six districts retained their same members, Edenton District reelected Jones and Hill; Wilmington District, Harnett and Ashe. The other members who retained their seats were Coor, Eaton and Person.

Such was the personnel of the Council that was to put into execution the measures of the Congress for the defense of the province. This was the most important business that came before Congress. Clinton with a large force of British regulars was at Cape Fear awaiting the arrival of Sir Peter Parker's fleet with Cornwallis's army. "Our whole time," wrote Thomas Jones, May 7, "has been taken up here in raising and arming men, and making every necessary military arrangement. The word is war, or as Virgil expresses it, *bella, horrida bella*. Two thousand ministerial troops are in Cape Fear, 5,000 more hourly expected; to oppose the whole will require a large force." [1]   The Congress, accordingly, in addition to the troops already in the field, ordered the levying of four continental regiments, the enlistment of three companies of light-horse, the drafting of 1,500 militia, and the organization into five companies of 415 independent volunteers. The light-horse were offered to the Continental Congress and accepted; the militia were ordered to Wilmington "for the protection of this province;" and the independent companies were directed to patrol the coast against the ravages of small armed vessels which were accustomed in this way to secure fresh supplies for the troops below Wilmington.

It was comparatively an easy matter to raise these troops; to clothe, feed and equip them was another problem. It is of course, unneces-

---

[1] Col. Rec., X, 1038.

sary to say that this was a problem that was
not solved at all during the Revolution, either
by the Continental Congress or by the North
Carolina Congress; but perhaps the latter came
as near to it as the former, or as any of the States.
This was the work in which Cornelius Harnett
was most actively concerned. In the Congress
at Halifax he served on committees to ascertain
the amount of gunpowder in the province; to
form an estimate of the expense of supporting
the troops; to draw up regulations for the com-
missary department; to devise measures for
defense of the coast; and to draft a form of
commission for privateers. But his most important work was on a committee "to take into
consideration the most practical and expeditious
method of supplying the province with arms,
ammunition, warlike stores and supplies, and also
the expediency of erecting works for the making
of saltpeter, gunpowder and purifying sulphur."
This committee recommended the erection at
Halifax of a plant for the manufacture of saltpeter; the erection somewhere in Halifax county
of a powder mill; the establishment of salt
works in various places; the erection of a gun
factory in each of the six military districts; and
the purchase or rental of certain furnaces and
iron works for casting pieces of ordnance, shot
and other warlike material. The report was
adopted by the Congress; how its provisions

were to be carried into execution was a matter
for the Council of Safety.   Their effectiveness
must be judged by their results.   Certainly
they fell short of what was desired, yet during
the summer of 1776, they saved North Carolina
from invasion, they enabled the troops of the
province to participate with credit in the defense
of Charleston, and they were sufficient to crush
the Indians on the western frontier.   If to these
results we add the overthrow of the Highlanders
at Moore's Creek Bridge, and the impetus given
to the cause of independence by the Resolution
of April 12th, it will appear that at least during
the spring and summer of 1776 North Carolina
was not backward in the common cause.

While these events were occurring, Cornelius
Harnett was at the head of the provisional
government.   We may almost say that they
occurred during his administration, for certainly
no man contributed more to these results than he.
In the Congress he served on more committees
concerned in devising measures of defense than
any other man.   He wrote the Resolution of
April 12th.   He was president of the Provincial
Council and of the Council of Safety to which
were entrusted the execution of ordinances and
the direction of armies, and as such he guided the
affairs of both with such a measure of success
that the enemy attributed to him more than to
any of his colleagues the downfall of the royal

government and the spirited conduct of the Revolutionary program. Referring to the work of the Halifax Congress, Governor Martin, writing in November from New York, says: "By a person who left North Carolina in the month of September last, I am informed the rebels in that colony were so infatuated with the idea of being an independent State, as declared by the Congress [April 12], that they have struck paper money with so liberal a hand, for the support of the war, as to have emitted £550,000, which vast sum was then [in September] nearly expended. The leaders of their politics at that time were Cornelius Harnett, Willie Jones, and Thomas Jones, who are all very guilty characters. * * * To what an extreme of madness is this People arrived!"[1]   More than a year before, Martin, as we have seen, had selected Harnett, Ashe, Howe and Nash as persons worthy of the king's special vengeance because they stood "foremost among the patrons of revolt and anarchy." Since then Howe's work in the field, and Harnett's work in the Council, had multiplied many times their score of offenses, and Martin treasured them up to be laid before the British commander upon his arrival in the province. Accordingly, on May 5, 1776, from the cabin of the *Pallisser*, as she rode at anchor in Cape Fear River below Wilmington, Sir Henry Clinton issued his proclamation declaring the colony in rebellion, and

---

[1] Col. Rec., X, 900.

stating that he had it in command from the king
to proceed against all men or bodies of men in
arms, and all congresses and committees "as
against open enemies of the State." However
before it was too late, he desired "from the principle of humanity" to forewarn the deluded
people of the miseries ever attendant upon
civil war, and to "entreat and exhort" them
"to appease the vengeance of an injured and
justly incensed Nation by a return to their duty
to our common sovereign, and to the blessings
of a free government as established by law."
To give them a last chance to do so, he offered
"in his Majesty's name free pardon to all such
as shall lay down their arms and submit to the
laws, excepting only from the benefits of such
pardon Cornelius Harnett and Robert Howes."[1]
"Cornelius Harnett," thus comments Frothingham, "was the foremost actor in the movement
for independency, and Howe, having accepted
a commission from the Provincial Congress,
was rendering noble service in the field." [2]   One
month later, June 5, the Council of Safety met
at Wilmington, and in reply to Clinton's proclamation unanimously elected Harnett president.[3]

---

[1] Col. Rec., X, 591—592. For this spelling of Robert Howe's name
see note p. 101.

[2] Rise of the Republic, 504.

[3] Harnett served until August 21, when he resigned and was succeeded by Samuel Ashe. Ashe resigned in September and was succeeded by Willie Jones. The Council was in session at Wilmington
from June 5 to 15 ; at the house of William Whitfield, on Neuse river,
near the present town of Kinston, from June 19 to July 16 ; at Halifax
from July 21 to August 13 ; at the house of Joel Lane, the site of the
present city of Raleigh, from August 21 to 28 ; at Salisbury from September 6 to September 13; at Halifax from September7 to 2 October 25.

An attempt to follow in detail the numerous problems presented for the consideration of President Harnett and his colleagues would doubtless make but a dull and lifeless narrative. Yet upon the proper disposition of these matters depended the execution of laws, the administration of justice, the preservation of order, and the success of armies; and when we consider these facts, we may well doubt whether in subordinating such details to more dramatic and striking events, the narrative does not lose in instructiveness what it may gain in interest. The fidelity with which the members of the Council attended to the details of these problems is a good index to their characters and patriotism. Nothing less than boundless faith in the justice of their cause and in its ultimate success could have sustained them in the discharge of their delicate and exacting duties. There was nothing in the character of their labor, such as the soldier finds in the excitement of the campaign, to lighten fatigue or banish anxiety. Nor were they, like the soldier, inspired by the hope of glory and renown; on the contrary their duties were of such a nature that to discharge them with fidelity and impartiality, would more likely invite criticism and denunciation than applause and popularity. There was no popular applause to be gained by even the strictest attention to the commonplace details incident to the detection, apprehension and punishment of rioters, counterfeiters, traitors and other malefactors. Little popularity was to be expected from efforts, however successful, to adjust disputes among army officers over their relative ranks; to pass impartially upon applications for military and civil commissions; to hear and determine justly appeals for pardon and prayers for mercy; to enforce rigid discipline among a mutinous soldiery; to execute martial law against former friends and neighbors whose only crime was refusal to join in rebellion and revolution; to enforce without an adequate police obedience to a confessedly revolutionary government among those who denied its moral or legal right to rule. Whatever glory was to be won by successful military achievements all knew well enough would go to the soldiers in the field, not to the councilors in the cabinet who, by grinding out their spirits and lives over details of organizing and equipping armies, made such success possible. Nevertheless, day and night, week in and week out, President Harnett and his associates with unfailing tact, patience and energy, and with remarkable success, gave conscientious and efficient attention to a thousand and one details as uninspiring as they were necessary. In the discharge of his duties as president, says McRee, "Harnett sustained himself with masterly ability, overcoming difficulties by his energy, illuminating perplexing

11

questions with the light of a disciplined and highly cultured intellect. He commanded the respect of all by his stability of purpose and dignity, and attached to himself by his fascinating address and power of persuasion a multitude of friends." [1]

The chief problems of the Council related to defense. [2] The Indians on the frontier, the Tories of the interior, and Clinton on the coast threatened the province with attack from three directions. A few days before the Council met, Clinton withdrew from the Cape Fear river, but nobody knew where he had gone nor what his plans were, and all apprehended that his movement was but a change of base for an attack on North Carolina. Clinton did contemplate such a movement, but was frustrated by the activity of the committees and the Council. The Council's problem was to organize and equip the troops ordered by the Congress. The organization was more tedious than difficult, but it required much time and labor. A harder task was to equip them. Even the utmost exertions of the Council could not keep the several arsenals sufficiently supplied to meet the constant calls on them for arms and ammunition. The Council continued to press into public service arms found in private hands; they appointed

---

[1] "Cornelius Harnett," in the Wilmington Chronicle, copied in the Raleigh Register, August 30, 1844.

[2] The proceedings of the Council are printed in Col. Rec., X, 618—647 ; 682—707 ; 826—830 ; 873—881.

commissioners to purchase warlike supplies; they imported them from other states; they manufactured them; they purchased them in the North through the delegates in the Continental Congress; and they chartered vessels which they loaded with cargoes of staves and shingles to be exchanged for military supplies. The *Polly*, the *Heart of Oak*, the *King Fisher*, the *Lilly*, the *Little Thomas*, the *Johnston*, and other fast sailing vessels slipped through the inlets of eastern Carolina, ran down to the West Indies, sold their cargoes of lumber, and eluding the British cruisers which patrolled those waters returned safely to Ocracoke, Edenton, and New Bern with cargoes of small arms, cannon, gunpowder, salt, clothes and shoes. Their enterprising crews, the prototypes of the more famous blockade-runners of later days, continued this work throughout the Revolution, and made no inconsiderable contributions to the cause of American independence. The Council issued letters of marque and reprisal to the *Pennsylvania Farmer*, the *King Tammany*, the *General Washington*, the *Heart of Oak*, and the *Johnston;* and they organized courts of admiralty and appointed judges. They set up iron works for casting cannon and shot, and salt works for supplying that necessary article. In one way or another they managed to put into the field equipped for service 1,400 splendid troops for the defense of Charleston, 300 militia for the aid of Virginia against the Indians, and an army of 2,500 rifle-men for a campaign against the Creeks and Cherokees beyond the Alleghanies.[1]

Cornelius Harnett inspired his colleagues with the same continental spirit that was the most striking characteristic of his own statesmanship and they brought to their task a breadth of view that recognized no boundary between colonies struggling in the common cause. Without hesi-tation they sent their continental troops and mili-tia into South Carolina for the defense of Charles-ton; and President Harnett assured President Rut-ledge that "this colony will upon all occasions afford South Carolina every possible assistance."[2] Troops, arms, ammunition and supplies, were poured into that colony with a liberality that "left this colony almost in a defenseless state, defenseless and very, very alarming, * * * as we have every reason to expect General Clinton's return here should he fail in his expe-dition against South Carolina."[3] Virginia, threatened by Indians on her western frontier, besought the North Carolina Council for aid, which was promptly supplied over the protest of their own commander in the western district.[4]

---

[1] This expedition was under the command of General Griffith Ruth-erford. It was "the greatest expedition ever sent against the Chero-kee," and was waged "with such distinguished success that both North Carolina and Tennessee have named counties in his [Rutherford's] honor." 19th Annual Report of the Bureau of American Ethnology, 1897–98, Part I, 205.

[2] State Rec., XI, 313.

[3] State Rec., XI, 299, 309.

[4] Col. Rec., X, 671, 680 ; State Rec., XI, 313.

South Carolina and Georgia both sought permission to recruit in North Carolina, and received from the Council not permission merely, but "every facility and assistance" in their work. "We have given every facility and assistance to the recruiting officers from the State of Georgia," wrote the Council to the North Carolina delegates in the Continental Congress, "and have the pleasure to acquaint you that they have met with great success." [1]   Indeed, so great was their success that John Penn thought it would "be prudent to stop the officers of the neighboring states from enlisting any more men in North Carolina until we have completed our quota."[2] Prudent it would undoubtedly have been, but prudence of such a nature as did not appeal to Cornelius Harnett and his associates of the Council. They cared little whether the men were enlisted under the banner of North Carolina, Virginia, South Carolina or Georgia, provided only they were under the banner of the United States. Consequently North Carolina became the "recruiting ground for the entire South," and many a soldier who followed the flag of another State thought, as he struck down his country's foes, of his little cabin nestling among the pines of the Old North State. It was the manifestation of this spirit that led Charles Pinckney, of South Carolina, referring to North

---

[1] State Rec., XI, 350.

[2] Col. Rec., X, 802.

Carolina's "zeal for the glorious cause in which
they are engaged," to declare with pardonable
exaggeration: "They have been so willing and
ready on all occasions to afford us all the assistance in their power, that I shall ever love a
North Carolinian, and join with Colonel Moul-
trie in confessing that they have been the salvation of this country." [1]

This work of the Council was done in spite
of a strong and energetic domestic enemy in
their own midst. The Tories of North Carolina,
as the Council declared, were "a numerous
body of people * * * who, although lately
subdued, are only waiting a more favorable
opportunity to wreak their vengeance upon us."
The Tories hoped and the Whigs feared that this
opportunity would come through a British
success either at Wilmington or at Charleston.
Moore's Creek Bridge had warned the former
of the folly of an uprising without the cooperation of the British army, and the result at Charleston dashed their hopes of an immediate insurrection. Nevertheless they regarded this as
only a temporary setback which necessitated
a postponement but not a surrender of their
plans. Though forced to work more quietly,
they seized every opportunity to undermine
and counteract the work of the Council. The
Council, therefore, were compelled to devote
a large part of their time to the detection and

---

[1] McCrady: South Carolina in the Revolution, 1775-1780, p. 314.

punishment of these domestic enemies. Their
active leaders were arrested and brought before
the Council on such general charges as denouncing the Council and the committees for exercising arbitrary and tyrannical powers; as uttering
"words inimical to the cause of liberty"; as
endeavoring "to inflame the minds of the
people against the present American measures";
as using their influence to prevent the people
from "associating in the common cause." More
specific charges were correspondence with the
enemy; refusal to receive the continental currency; and efforts to depreciate both the continental and provincial bills of credit. The
Council dealt with each case upon its individual
merits. In a general way, however, they permitted those who were willing to subscribe
the test and submit to the Revolutionary government to remain at home unmolested. They
"naturalized" prisoners captured in battle who
expressed a willingness to take the oath of allegiance, and admitted them to the privileges
of free citizens. Persons suspected of disaffection, but who had committed no overt act,
were required to give bond for their good behavior.
Those whose presence among their neighbors
was regarded as dangerous were taken from
their homes and paroled within prescribed
limits; while the most active leaders were imprisoned, some in North Carolina, some in Virginia

and some in Philadelphia. The last two methods
of punishment in some cases worked real hardships and moving appeals were made to President
Harnett for relaxations of the restrictions.

While a majority of the cases that came before
the Council involved the conduct of individuals
only, a few instances were reported in which
something like general disaffection appeared in
a community. In such cases the Council acted
with determination and vigor. Those who
they thought were led into disaffection through
ignorance they undertook to instruct in "their
duty to Almighty God," and to "the United
States of America." But to those "who had been
nursed up in the very bosom of the country,"
and yet "by their pretended neutrality declare
themselves enemies to the American Union,"
the Council offered but one course,—the
pledge either of their property or their persons
for their good behavior. On July 4, 1776, they
directed the county committees to require under
oath from all suspected persons inventories of
their estates, and ordered the commanding
officers of the militia to arrest all who refused
and bring them before the Council for trial.
This order going forth simultaneously with the
news of Clinton's defeat at Charleston, carried
dismay into the ranks of the Loyalists. "This
glorious news [Clinton's defeat], with the resolve
of Council against the Tories," wrote James

Davis, the public printer, "has caused a very great commotion among them. They are flocking in to sign the test and association."[1] By these vigorous measures the Council dealt Toryism in North Carolina a serious blow, and saved the province during the summer of 1776 from the horrors of civil war. It must of course be confessed that these measures, though taken in the name of liberty, smacked themselves of tyranny; their justification lies in the fact that they were in behalf of peace and the rights of mankind.

On July 22d, while the Council were in session at Halifax, came the welcomed news that the Continental Congress had adopted a Declaration of Independence. The Council received the news with great joy. No longer rebellious subjects in arms against their sovereign, they were now the leaders of a free people in their struggle for constitutional self-governm ent. The Council, therefore, immediately resolved that by the Declaration of Independence the people "were absolved from all allegiance to the British Crown," and therefore "the test as directed to be subscribed by the Congress at Halifax [was] improper and nugatory." The first clause of this test—"We the subscribers professing our allegiance to the king, and acknowledging the constitutional executive power of government"— was accordingly stricken out, and the amended

[1] Col. Rec., X, 666.

test, which contained no allusion to the king, was signed. The first person in North Carolina formally and irrevocably to abjure allegiance to the British Crown was Cornelius Harnett, whose name headed the list of the councilors who subscribed this new test.[1]

At Halifax the people of North Carolina gave the first official utterance in favor of a national declaration of independence. Cornelius Harnett was their mouthpiece. At Halifax the Declaration of Independence was first officially proclaimed to the people of North Carolina. Again, Cornelius Harnett was their mouthpiece. One incident was the logical outcome of the other, and the two together enriched our annals with a dramatic story. The first entry in the Council's journal for July 22, is a resolution requiring the committees throughout the State upon receiving the Declaration of Independence to "cause the same to be proclaimed in the most public manner in order that the good people of this colony may be fully informed thereof."[2] The Council set the example, and set apart Thursday, August 1, "for proclaiming the said Declaration at the court-house in the town of Halifax; the freeholders and inhabitants of the county of Halifax are requested to give their attendance at the time and place aforesaid."[3]

---

[1] Col. Rec., X, 684.
[2] Col. Rec., X, 682.
[3] Col. Rec., X, 688.

The people were profoundly interested. On the first day of August an "immense concourse of people" gathered in the county town to hear the official proclamation of their independence. "It is needless to say that * * * no question was raised as to who should read the great document. There was one man and only one whose name in every hamlet in North Carolina stood as the supreme embodiment of independence. Hardly four months had passed since he had read his own immortal declaration, and the declaration which he was now to read was but the enactment by a Continental Congress of what he had proposed to a Provincial Congress."[1] It is true that in substance the two documents were pretty much the same, but how different the circumstances under which Cornelius Harnett proclaimed them! On April 12th, he was a pioneer breaking the way with "the colonies from New England to Virginia in solid array" against him; on August 1st, he proclaimed the utterance of a united continent. The ceremony was simple enough. At noon the militia proudly paraded in such uniforms as they could boast, and with beating drums and flying flags escorted the Council to the court-house. The crowd cheered heartily as President Harnett ascended the platform. When the cheers had died away he arose and midst a profound silence read to the people the "Unanimous Declaration of the Thirteen United

---

[1] Smith : U. N. C. Mag., May, 1907, 393.

States of America." As he closed with the ringing words pledging to the support of that Declaration their lives, their fortunes, and their sacred honor, the people with shouts of joy gave popular ratification to the solemn pledge their representatives had made for them. In the exuberance of their enthusiasm the soldiers seized President Harnett and, forgetful of his staid dignity, bore him on their shoulders through the crowded street, applauding him as their champion and swearing allegiance to American Independence.[1]

Since the State was now independent it was advisable that a permanent form of government should displace the provisional government as soon as possible. Accordingly on the 9th of August, the Council of Safety resolved "that it be recommended to the good people of this now independent State of North Carolina to pay the greatest attention to the election to be held on the 15th day of October next, of delegates to represent them in Congress, and to have particularly in view this important consideration: that it will be the business of the delegates then chosen not only to make laws for the good government of, but also to form a Constitution for this State, that this last, as it is the corner-stone of all law, so it ought to be fixed and permanent, and that according as it is well or ill ordered,

---

[1] Jones : Defense of North Carolina, 268—269.

it must tend in the first degree to promote the happiness or the misery of the State." [1]

A campaign famous for its violence followed. Democracy exulting in a freedom too newly acquired for it to have learned the virtue of self-restraint, struck blindly and fiercely to right and left and inflicted upon some of the sturdiest champions of constitutional government wounds that time itself could never heal. Among those who fell before this onslaught was Samuel Johnston who had so long tempered the proceedings of the Congress with his wise conservatism. His seat was filled by some worthy of whom history takes no account. However he still exercised a powerful influence in the deliberations of the Convention, for some of his warmest friends and supporters won seats in that body. One of these was William Hooper who was returned from Wilmington. Cornelius Harnett was so anxious that Hooper should be in the Convention that he relinquished his hold on that borough in Hooper's favor, and himself stood for election in Brunswick county. Brunswick returned him second in her delegation, immediately after Maurice Moore, her own favorite son. The Convention met at Halifax November 12th. Richard Caswell was elected president. Harnett was delayed in reaching Halifax, and did not arrive until two days after the organization of the Convention. [2]

---

[1] Col. Rec., X, 696.

[2] The proceedings are printed in Col. Rec., X, 913—1003.

Immediately after organizing, the Convention appointe a committee to frame "a Bill of Rights and form of a Constitution for the government of this State." [1] Harnett was a member of this committee. The debates on the Constitution have not been preserved and contemporary documents bearing on the subject are few and meager. But little, therefore, is known of the contributions made to it by individuals, and that little is chiefly a matter of tradition rather than of record. Tradition, supported by an occasional contemporary record, attributes to Harnett a large share in the shaping of the Constitution. His contributions present him in the characteristic role of opposing religious and intellectual bigotry, and advocating a broader political freedom. He threw himself vigorously against the efforts of Samuel Johnston and his immediate followers to secure the establishment of the Church of England as part of the new State government. Tradition ascribes to him the authorship and adoption of the thirty-ninth article which declared "that there shall be no establishment of any one religious church or denomination in this State in preference to any other, but all persons shall be at liberty to exercise their own mode of worship." In keeping with this spirit was his attitude toward the famous thirty-second article. As originally

---

1 The Bill of Rights and Constitution are printed in Col. Rec., X, 1003—1013.

drawn by Thomas Jones this article declared any person incapable of holding any office of trust or profit in the State who denied "the truth of the Protestant Episcopal Church or religion." Harnett led the fight against this clause, but prejudice against the Roman Catholic Church was so strong that he could do no more than secure the rejection of the words "Episcopal Church." [1] More than half a century passed before religious toleration in the State reached the point where the word "Protestant" was discarded for the broader term "Christian," and a still longer period, before Harnett's views prevailed and the Constitution was purged altogether of religious bigotry. In 1776 such views were regarded as so extremely liberal that strict sectarians among his contemporaries thought of Harnett as little better than an infidel.

Perhaps the most difficult task connected with the formation of the Constitution was to define the powers of the governor. Under the royal government neither the people nor the Assembly exercised any constitutional control over the governor. They had no voice in his appointment; they held no restraints over his conduct; they had no means of removing him if he proved unfit. His authority was neither fixed nor definite. He acted under instructions from the

1 MS. letter of Jo. Seawell Jones to William Gaston, April 7, 1834. His information, he declares, was "founded upon a somewhat intimate acquaintance with the private papers of those who formed the Constitution of North Carolina." Also McRee's article on Cornelius Harnett in the Raleigh Register, August 30, 1844.

Crown, whose representative he was, and these instructions he could not make public except by special permission. As the personal representative of the Crown he was apt to entertain extravagant ideas of his prerogatives and to aim at the utmost extension of his authority. The Assembly struggled hard to hedge him about with all sorts of restrictions, and the result was a perpetual conflict between the executive and legislative branches of the government with every advantage in favor of the former. In consequence of this system the people felt hampered in the only branch of the government in which they had a direct share, and chafed impatiently under the restriction. Accordingly when they came, under the leadership of Cornelius Harnett, to define the powers of their chief executive in the new State government, they were in a decidedly reactionary frame of mind. "What powers, sir," inquired one of Hooper's constituents, "were conferred on the governor?" "Power," replied Hooper, "to sign a receipt for his salary." In truth the legislative branch now had the upper hand and the pendulum swung to the other extreme. Not only was the governor shorn of most of his most important powers; with every power conferred on him the Constitution coupled a restriction. He could take no important step without the advice and consent of the Council of State, and in the selection of the councilors he had no voice. But the Council exercised a restraining authority only; to the governor belonged the right of initiative and this fact, coupled with the moral influence of the office, gave the incumbent opportunity for great service and usefulness to the State. Nevertheless, an active, aggressive and resourceful executive was apt to become restive under the restraints. Governor Caswell, for instance, when urged by Cornelius Harnett to pursue a more aggressive policy in the prosecution of the war, retorted that his hands were tied, and that no man was so much responsible for it as Cornelius Harnett himself. Harnett had urged that "spirited measures" be adopted to fill up the State's regiments for the spring campaign of 1778. "My good friend, Mr. Harnett,'' replied Caswell, in a letter addressed to Penn and Harnett, "knows that by the Constitution of this State, nothing can be done by the executive power of itself towards this most desirable purpose and that the General Assembly is not to meet until the month of April. Of course ways and means can not be fallen on to accomplish what he hopes in time to render that service to the common cause he and I both wish, and I think if there is any blame to be fixed on those who formed the Constitution a very considerable part he ought to take to him-

12

self for cramping so much the powers of the executive." [1]

The Constitution directed that the Assembly at its first session after each annual election should elect a governor, and other officials, and seven councilors of State. In order to bridge the gap between the adjournment of the Congress and the meeting of the first Assembly, a temporary provision was made by the adoption of an ordinance appointing Richard Caswell governor; James Glasgow secretary of State; Cornelius Harnett, Thomas Person, William Dry, William Haywood, Edward Starkey, Joseph Leech, and Thomas Eaton councilors of State. Three days later, December 23, the Congress adjourned.[2] The new state officials met at New Bern in January, and took the oath of office on January 16th. Cornelius Harnett was elected president of the Council.[3] The first Assembly under the Constitution met at New Bern, April 7th, 1777, and reelected all the above officials except Dry and Person, whose places were filled with William Cray and William Taylor.[4] But Cornelius Harnett was not to serve longer on the Council. On May 1st, before his new term began, the Assembly elected him a delegate to the Continental Congress.

[1] State Rec., XIII, 31.
[2] Col. Rec., X, 1013.
[3] State Rec., XI, 363 ; XXII, 906—909.
[4] State Rec., XII, 24—25, 27.

X

IN THE CONTINENTAL CONGRESS

Harnett was not a candidate for the Continental Congress. Had the Assembly been guided by his wishes they would not have elected him; had he consulted his own good he would not have accepted. But the circumstances under which he was elected were such that a decent regard for his duty as a citizen forbade his declining, and to the voice of public duty he had not yet learned to turn a deaf ear. When the Assembly met it was soon found that the factions into which the last two congresses had divided had grown into parties. Fundamental differences lay at their roots, and never again in the history of North Carolina was there to be that political harmony and unanimity on public matters which had prevailed in the congresses of 1774 and 1775. Among the prominent leaders of the Conservatives was Joseph Hewes, a delegate in the Continental Congress and a candidate for reelection. The Radicals brought out John Penn to oppose him. "A warm struggle," wrote Abner Nash, "is likely to take place between Mr. Penn and Mr. Hewes for a seat in Congress."[1] It was indeed a "warm struggle," characterized by much hard feeling. Penn won. With him were elected Thomas Burke and William Hooper.

---

[1] State Rec., XI, 453.

The result was a bitter pill to Hewes and his friends. "Hewes," wrote Johnston, "was supplanted of his seat in Congress by the most insidious arts and glaring falsehoods, and Hooper, though no competitor appeared to oppose him, lost a great number of votes."[1] Hooper declined to accept, and a bad situation was thus made worse. Prudence dictated the election of some man upon whom both parties could unite and whose choice would quiet the ruffled waters. Of the prominent politicians at that time there were probably but two whose election would answer that end. One had just been elected governor, and was, therefore, not to be considered. The other was Cornelius Harnett. To Harnett, accordingly, the Assembly turned, and under such circumstances he could do nothing but acquiesce in the Assembly's wishes. Elected May 1, 1777, he was reelected April 25, 1778, and again May 8, 1779.[2] The Articles of Confederation, ratified by North Carolina April 24, 1778, forbade any delegate's serving in the Continental Congress more than three years in any six successive years. Accordingly, at the close of his third term in Congress, Harnett retired to private life.

As soon as possible after his election, Harnett set out for Philadelphia where he arrived on

---

[1] MS. letter in the library at "Hayes." Copy in the collections of the North Carolina Historical Commission. See also McRee's Life and Correspondence of James Iredell, I, 358.

[2] State Rec., XII, 65—67,602—608, 711—718 ; XIII, 754—756, 808—811.

July 18th. He took his seat in Congress on the 22d. The next three years were the least satisfactory years of his long public career. Nominally a seat in Congress was the highest honor that a free State could confer on one of its citizens; practically it meant loss of political influence and preferment. The Continental Congress had lost much of its early prestige. Many of the eminent leaders who had given it distinction and power had retired from its halls to the councils of their own states, to foreign courts, and to the battlefield. These now offered greater opportunities for service and distinction than Congress. Still there was important work for Congress to do. The Articles of Confederation were to be completed. The army was to be maintained. The navy was to be created, organized and manned. In the name of Congress, American ministers were received at foreign courts. By its authority they negotiated treaties. Upon its credit they borrowed money. But at home the authority of Congress was merely nominal. The states themselves no longer treated its decrees with respect, nor its requisitions with obedience. Harnett soon found that his opportunity for serving the State was extremely narrow and cramped. His situation was disagreeable and harassing in the extreme, his health was poor, and his expenses great. He missed the comforts of home, suffered the tortures of gout,

wearied of the sectional jealousies of North and
South, heard with impatience the quarrels and
bickerings of Congress, until he was thoroughly
worn out. A high sense of public duty alone
held him to his disagreeable post, for he declared
that although anxious to be relieved, yet as long
as his country desired his services he would
give them to the best of his ability "either with
or without pay."

The truth is Harnett entered the Continental
Congress too late to add to his own fame or to
render any conspicuous service to his country.
His career in Congress is of interest even to his
biographer not so much for what he did as for
what he wanted done. For this we must search
not the journals of Congress, but his public
and private correspondence. A delegate to the
Continental Congress partook somewhat of the
nature of a minister from one government to
another. His chief duty was to keep his own
government informed on the general situation
and to suggest measures for the general good.
None of the letters written by the North Carolina
delegates are more interesting or suggestive
than Harnett's. "No true North Carolinian,"
wrote Governor Swain, "will read his public
letters without increased respect and affection
for the State and without very high admiration
of the courage which sustained the writer in the
darkest days of the Revolution, and the lofty

and disinterested patriotism exhibited throughout the whole course of his legislative career." [1] These letters reveal a clear insight into the general situation and are punctured throughout with sensible, pointed suggestions. Addressed to his own State, his appeals in behalf of the common cause are both forcible and eloquent.

The policies that Harnett recommended were the ones so plainly marked out by the demands of the situation that it is astonishing to find they were not followed. He urged the State to keep her continental regiments well filled that Washington might find himself always in command of "a formidable army in the field well provided and well equipped." "We are daily entertained," he wrote, "by members of Congress with paragraphs of letters giving an account of the surprising exertions of their constituents. I beg that you will inform me what has been done by our General Assembly in this way. We have often been before them; I hope we shall never be behind them." [2] He besought Burke to inform him "of the temper you find our Assembly in. Are they inclined to pursue spirited measures? For God's sake, fill up your battalions, lay taxes, put a stop to the sordid and avaricious spirit which [has] affected all ranks and conditions of men."[3] He begged the State to fortify her seacoast.

---

[1] U. N. C. Mag., X, 337.
[2] State Rec., XI, 694.
[3] State Rec., XI, 696.

But he was almost alone in understanding the advantage which England's navy gave her over a people without naval power and with a long defenseless coast. "God send our Assembly may have wisdom enough to fortify their seaports," he exclaimed. "I am distressed beyond measure," he wrote to Governor Caswell, "to find our seacoast so much neglected." Again and again he recurred to the subject, but all to no purpose. The Assembly did nothing. "Mr. Maclaine writes me," he wrote, "he had hopes of getting our river [Cape Fear] fortified, but I have despaired of it long ago; if the Assembly should agree to it, I shall believe that miracles have not yet ceased." [1]   But miracles had ceased so far as the Assembly gave any evidence to the contrary. The people's representatives saved their constituents' money, but they paid the price in blood and suffering. Harnett urged that taxes be levied to keep up the credit of the continental and provincial currency. In a letter to Burke, suggesting matters for the consideration of the Assembly, he declared: "That of taxation is essential above all. The credit of our continental currency depends upon it." "This measure of taxation," he wrote to the governor, "unless entered into with spirit by the legislatures of the several states must end in the ruin of the prodigious quantity of paper money now in circulation." He earnestly desired to

[1] State Rec., XI, 590, 825 ; XIII, 21—22, 361.

put a stop to the Philadelphia printing presses
which were turning out millions of depreciated
bills of credit. "Congress," he wrote, "seem
determined to put a stop to the further emissions
of money. I wish they may be able to accomplish this desirable end." [1]   But this could not
be done because Congress had no power to levy
taxes and the states would not exercise their
taxing power to supply the continental treasury.
Harnett denounced in no uncertain terms the
greed of those who took advantage of the unfortunate condition of their country to reap wealth
for themselves. "The villainous practice of
raising the price of all the necessaries and con-
veniences of life," he declared, "is spreading all
over the continent. * * * America has more
to apprehend from the consequences of this
avaricious spirit than from two such armies as
General Howe's." [2] He warned the people against
the folly of expecting foreign powers to win
their independence for them and declared that
they must depend upon their own valor and
patriotism. "The independence of America is,
we think, secured by Spain's entering into the
war, and nothing remains for us to do but to
keep a good army in the field and support the
public credit," but he instantly added, "this
depends solely upon the patriotic exertions of
the several states." "All our foreign intelligence,"

---

[1] State Rec., XI, 694, 819, 696 ; XIV, 348.
[2] State Rec., XI, 749, 762, 780, 786, 820.

he declared at another time, "indicates that Europe will soon be in a flame. Let us not depend upon this. If we have virtue, we certainly have power to work out our own salvation, I hope without fear or trembling." [1] He saw the necessity for a stronger union between the states, and was always ready to support any member of the Confederacy against the common enemy. Urging his own State to make every exertion to aid Georgia and South Carolina, he declared: "I am one of those old politicians who had much rather see my neighbor's house on fire than my own, but at the same time would lend every assistance in my power to quench the flame." [2]

This sentence is a succinct statement of the policy which he pursued toward the Articles of Confederation. His votes on the Articles reveal in him a thoroughgoing state rights man, yet he believed thoroughly in an effective and efficient union of the states. "Every member of Congress," he declared, "seems to wish for a Confederacy except my good friend Burke, who laughs at it as a chimerical project; it does not strike me in that point of view. I think that unless the states confederate a door will be left open for continental contention and bloodshed, and that very soon after we are at peace with Europe."[3]

---

[1] State Rec., XI, 696 ; XIII, 21, 304 ; XIV, 206.

[2] State Rec., XIII, 224, 305 ; XIV, 190, 205.

[3] State Rec., XIII, 386.

But the union that he advocated was not to be a Nation of individuals, but a Confederacy of sovereign states. He opposed every effort of the larger states to secure population as the basis of representation in Congress, and supported the clause that gave to each State but a single vote. He stood with the state rights party in reserving to the states the power of taxation and the power of regulating commerce. He favored the clause that forbade Congress to make any treaty with a foreign power which should interfere with the right of any State to levy such duties as were imposed upon its own citizens. In apportioning the quota to be paid by each State into the Continental treasury, he favored the assessment of all property in general, in preference to the poll or the assessed value of real estate. He voted against the proposal to erect into a national domain the vast territory lying between the Alleghanies and the Mississippi to which Virginia, North Carolina and other states laid claim.[1] These votes illustrate his position, and it is not necessary to pursue the subject in further detail. It is not probable that Harnett contributed much, or anything to the final shaping of the Articles. They were already too far advanced when he entered Congress, and were adopted shortly after he took his seat. The final vote was

---

[1] Ford : Journals of the Continental Congress ; State Rec., XI, 648, 696, 814.

taken on November 15th. Two days before,
Harnett wrote to Burke: "The child Congress
has been big with these two years past is at last
brought forth—Confederation. I fear it will
by several legislatures be thought a little de-
formed; you will think it a monster. I wish,
however, some kind of confederation would take
place. Some carry their idea of this matter
so far as to believe our affairs must be ruined
without it. Be this as it may, it will in a few
days be sent to the legislatures of the several
states." [1]   He regarded it as "the most difficult
piece of business that ever was undertaken
by any public body," and thought it "the best
confederacy that could be formed especially
when we consider the number of states, their
different interests, [and] customs." [2]   Harnett
was very solicitous as to the fate of the Articles
in North Carolina, but apparently without
cause. They were laid before the Legislature
April 24th, and were promptly ratified. [3]   Governor Caswell's letter enclosing a copy of the
Legislature's resolution was laid before the
Continental Congress May 18th,[4] but it was not
until July 21st that John Penn signed the Confederation in behalf of North Carolina. Harnett
who had been on a visit to North Carolina

---

[1] State Rec., XI, 677.
[2] State Rec., XI, 814.
[3] State Rec., XII, 708, 717.
[4] Ford : Journals of the Continental Congress.

returned to Congress August 10th, and later attached his signature.

Harnett was not politically ambitious. Public office as such made no appeal to him. He did not need its emoluments. He cared little for its distinctions. Indeed, the offices which he held brought more of sacrifice than of gain, more of drudgery than of glory. Desire to serve his country regardless of cost to himself alone held him to the duties and burdens of his "very disagreeable and troublesome office." He had been in Philadelphia but a short time when he was struck with amazement "at the most extravagant prices" at which all kinds of articles were selling and discovered that his salary of $1,800 was not sufficient to meet his expenses.[1] He begged his friend Burke not to bring his wife to York, Pa., where Congress was sitting. "I should be very sorry," he wrote, "to see my countrywoman in distress, which be assured, must be the case if you bring her here. No, my friend, let her remain at your own peaceful mansion in expectation of better times. * * * I never lived in so wretched a manner in my life. I shall be under the necessity of procuring in advance from the treasury at least $1000 over and above my allowance from the State which is very handsome. I shall be content if this will bring me home with a single dollar in my pocket. Mention not this; if you do I am sure

---

1 State Rec., XI, 749.

you will not be believed, but it is as true as the gospel. God only knows what this country will come to at last."[1]   At another time he wrote: "I shall return [to North Carolina] indebted to my country at least £6000, [for advances from the treasury over and above his salary], and you very well know how we live. Do not mention this complaint to any person. I am content to sit down with this loss and much *more* if my country requires it."[2]   But when he found that these sacrifices were required without bringing adequate compensation in the way of service to the State, the burden of his position became intolerable. The honor staled. The incapacity of Congress wearied and disgusted him. "Congress," he wrote, "seems to go on in the old way, sometimes disputing upon trifles and neglecting the greater matters of the law," "doing more in three hours at one time than they do at another in three days."[3]   To his business partner at Wilmington, William Wilkinson, he declared: "If I once more can return to my family all the devils in hell shall not separate us. The honor of being once a member of Congress is sufficient for me; I acknowledge it is the highest honor a free State can bestow on one of its members. I shall be careful to ask for nothing more, but will sit down under my own vine and my own fig tree (for I have them both)

---

[1] State Rec., XI, 697.
[2] State Rec., XIV, 348.
[3] State Rec., XIII, 470, 483.

at Poplar Grove where none shall make me
afraid except the boats of the British cruisers."[1]
In a letter to Governor Caswell he declared that
he would return to his home in April, 1778,
after being absent from his family for ten months,
and that he had "neither expectation nor wish
to return again, as I am convinced there will be
many candidates for the honorable employment;
I am not one, though I shall think it my duty
to serve my country to the best of my poor
abilities, either with or without pay." [2]

What "all the devils in hell" could not do,
Harnett's patriotism did. In April, 1778, he
visited his family and at the desire of the Assembly returned to Congress in August. January
of 1779 brought another opportunity to return
to North Carolina. "After one of the most
terrible journeys that a man 55 years old ever
took," he declared, in the course of which he
"rode through frost and snow in some places
three feet deep," he reached Halifax January
22, where he found the Assembly in session.[3]
The next day the Senate proposed that a joint
committee of the two houses "be appointed for
the purpose of preparing the thanks of this State
to the Honorable Cornelius Harnett, Esquire,
one of the delegates for this State in the Continental Congress, for his faithful and important
services rendered this State in the execution of

---

1 State Rec., XI, 827.
2 State Rec., XIII, 385.
3 State Rec., XIV, 254.

that office." The House of Commons at once concurred, but added the names of the other delegates. Accordingly the speaker returned the thanks of the State in suitable words, to which Harnett and John Williams responded in behalf of the delegates.[1]   On May 8th the Assembly for the third time elected Harnett to the Continental Congress, and on the 26th of July, sinking all personal considerations, he returned to his duties. Under the Articles of Confederation he could not succeed himself, and as the year drew to its close and the prospects of returning to the comforts of home drew near, something of his old spirits revived and found reflection in his letters. In February, 1780, he made his last journey from Philadelphia to Wilmington. From his quiet home at "Poplar Grove near Wilmington," on Washington's birthday, he wrote to Burke then at Philadelphia: "After one of the most fatiguing and most disagreeable journeys that ever [an] old fellow took, I at last arrived at my little hovel and had the happiness to find my family in good health." [2]   "I am very glad," his friend replied, "that you have surmounted the difficulties of a journey which I have often thought of with very great and severe apprehensions. Your spirits, I perceive, are good, and your health, I hope will always continue as well as you can wish it." [3]

---

[1] State Rec., XIII. 552, 653, 671-73.
[2] State Rec., XV, 341.
[3] State Rec., XV, 367.

XI

THE LAST YEAR

In his letters Harnett calls himself an old man. "I am *too* old to be sent here," he declared. "I am now not many years from sixty."[1] In reality, he was then only fifty-five, and when he retired from Congress he was but in his fifty-seventh year. We should not now call him an old man. But as Nicolay and Hay, in their "Abraham Lincoln," say: "In the latter half of the last century [the 18th] and the first half of this [the 19th], men were called old whom we should regard as in the prime of life." After citing illustrations of the statement, they continue: "The sober fact is that the life was a hard one, with few rational pleasures, few wholesome appliances. The strong ones lived, and some even attained great length of years; but to the many age came early and was full of infirmity and pain." Of the twenty-one delegates sent by North Carolina to the Continental Congress, the average age at death was fifty-nine years. One-third died before reaching fifty; more than half were under sixty; and but six reached three score and ten. The truth is, many a civilian, who is popularly supposed to have reposed in

---

1 State Rec., XIII, 305.

some safe and easy political berth, through the sacrifices, hardships, and the strain of harassing responsibilities, laid down his life in the cause of his country as literally as the soldier who fell on the field of battle. Certainly this is true of Cornelius Harnett. Deprived of the comforts of home, burdened with the responsibilities of a disagreeable office, and threatened with financial ruin, his indomitable spirit would still have sustained him under it all had not disease laid its heavy hand upon him. Much of his most arduous work was done in company with his "old companion," the gout, and many a lengthy official communication was written when it gave him "great pain to hold a pen" in his hand. As a result old age came to him early in life, and when he retired from Congress he was a physical wreck, broken in body and prematurely old.

Cornelius Harnett spent the last year of his life midst the gloom of repeated disaster. The summer of 1780 was the gloomiest period of the war in the South. In rapid succession Charleston fell, Buford's Virginians were cut to pieces at Waxhaws, and the enemy seized Augusta, Ninety-six, Camden, and other strategic points of the interior. The fall of Charleston carried with it the whole of Lincoln's army, including North Carolina's continental line and a thousand of her militia. After the disaster at Waxhaws,

"not a vestige of an American army was left
in all South Carolina." Georgia and South
Carolina were quickly overrun and North Carolina lay open to invasion without an organized
force to protect her soil or defend her honor.
The government strained every nerve, and
before Cornwallis was ready to advance had a
respectable force in the field. Then Gates came,
crowned with the laurels of Saratoga, and led
his army to the worst defeat recorded in American
annals. After Camden Cornwallis marched with
ease to Charlotte. King's Mountain and Cow-
pens brought rays of light in the general gloom,
but they were immediately followed by Greene's
retreat. Through the perspective of a hundred
and thirty years, we now see this great retreat
in its true light, but the patriots of 1780 saw
only Greene's ragged troops flying before the
pursuing foe, and it appeared to them but the
climax of a disastrous year.

The opening of the year 1781 brought the war
to Harnett's own door. In January, Major
James H. Craige, with an insignificant force
of British regulars, sailed up the Cape Fear and
occupied Wilmington without opposition. Craige
was a bold and aggressive soldier. His appear-
ance on the Cape Fear animated the spirits
of the Tories and dashed the hopes of the Whigs.
For four years the latter had slept in fancied
security, heedless of Harnett's warnings, as if

they expected the victories of 1776 to be a perpetual safeguard against attack. Craige gave them a rude awakening, and forced their leaders to abandon their homes and to seek refuge in obscure retreats in the country. But flight could not save them from the restless energy and bold activity of the British troopers, who made the life of every prominent Whig in eastern Carolina insecure.

Cornelius Harnett fell an early victim to their zeal. Proscribed by Governor Martin and outlawed by Sir Henry Clinton, he was the most shining mark upon which Craige could display his zeal in his master's cause. His first expedition after occupying Wilmington was organized for the capture of Harnett. Warned of his danger, Harnett attempted flight. He carried with him a considerable sum of public money with which he had been entrusted for the purchase of military supplies and clothing, and this he succeeded in conveying to a place of safety. But he himself, suddenly seized with a paroxysm of the gout, was compelled to seek relief at the home of a friend, Colonel James Spicer, in Onslow county, about thirty miles from Wilmington, where he was captured. Tortured with pain and utterly helpless, his hands and feet tightly bound, he was strapped across the back of a trooper's horse, and thus taken into Wilmington. The sight made a profound impression on those who beheld it. An interested spectator was

Armand John DeRosset, a boy of fourteen years, afterwards a well-known physician. His granddaughter refers to the incident in these words:[1] "One horrible recollection that remained with grandpa as long as he lived, was the sight of Cornelius Harnett (the idolized patriot of the Cape Fear), 'brought through the town, thrown across a horse like a sack of meal,' by a squad of Craige's marauders. * * * Driven before them, he had fallen in his tracks from exhaustion and in an unconscious state, was thus inhumanly treated." At Wilmington, by Craige's orders, he was thrown into a roofless blockhouse where he was exposed to all the inclemencies of the winter season. His strength gave way rapidly and it soon became evident that his end was near. Then Whigs and Tories alike prayed Craige for a relaxation of his severity, and the British commander yielded so far as to grant his dying prisoner a parole within the limits of the town.

But this clemency came too late. On April 28th, 1781, with his own hand, Harnett wrote his will in these words: "I give, devise and bequeath to my dear, beloved wife Mary, all my estate, real, personal, and mixed, of what nature or kind soever, to her, her heirs and assigns forever;" to which he added this codicil: "I, Cornelius Harnett, having executed the within written will, think it not improper to

---

[1] Catherine DeRosset Meares : Annals of the DeRosset Family, 50.

14

add that, as I have ever considered expensive
funerals as ostentatious folly it is my earnest
request (and from my present circumstances
now doubly necessary) that I may be buried
with the utmost frugality."[1] His last moments
are thus described by Hooper: "Aware that his
disease must terminate fatally, he declined the
advice of his physicians, but thankfully received
their kind and friendly attentions. In the last
stage of pain and suffering he had, as might
be expected, his moments of impatience and
asperity. The placidity of his temper never,
however, deserted him long; and he enjoyed a
serenity of mind to the last hour of his existence.
Some of his friends endeavored to present to his
mind the consolations of revealed religion and
to enforce on it the necessity of repentance;
but he had so entrenched himself in the positions
of infidelity that their approaches were too
easily resisted at that awful period. He died in
the tenets in which he had lived, and dictated
a short time before his expiration the simple
epitaph which appears above his grave,"[2]—the
following couplet from Pope's *Essay on Man:*

" Slave to no sect, he took no private road,
    But looked through Nature up to Nature's God."

Death came to him April 28th, 1781, in the
fifty-eighth year of his life. His body lies buried

---

[1] The original is preserved in the Court-house of New Hanover
county.

[2] U. N. C. Mag., IX, 334—335.

in the northeast corner of St. James' church-
yard in the city of Wilmington. A rude stone,
on which his epitaph is rudely and incorrectly
carved,[1] alone marks his final resting place;
but near by stands a granite shaft erected to his
memory by the grateful descendants of those
for whom he gave the last full measure of devotion.[2]

Hooper's statement, above quoted, classing
Harnett as an atheist, should not be passed
without comment. Hooper merely repeats a
tradition that sprang up a few years after Harnett's death and was accepted without question
by historians until the recent publication of
Harnett's letters and other papers. No one can
read these documents and accept Hooper's
statement as a fact. It is true that Harnett
lived in an age of speculation,—the age of
Thomas Paine, Benjamin Franklin and Thomas
Jefferson. Perhaps his fondness for speculative
philosophy at times led him to discourse in a
vein not altogether in harmony with the orthodox
religious views of those among whom he lived.
As Dr. Smith says: "Utterly unwarranted infer-
ences have been drawn from the couplet which
Harnett asked to be placed on his tomb."[3] In this
connection, it is interesting to note that at the
public sale of Governor Josiah Martin's property,

---

[1] The date of his death is given as April 20, 1781.
[2] Erected by the North Carolina Society of the Colonial Dames of
America, in 1907.
[3] U. N. C. Mag., May, 1907, note, 402.

sold by order of Congress at New Bern, February 6, 1777, Harnett made one purchase,—a book called "The Religion of Nature." [1] But while he nowhere gives expression to his religious views, he frequently refers to the Deity in words which no atheist could use and in a spirit totally foreign to atheism. Moreover with the shadow of death already darkening his countenance, he writes as the opening words of his will: "In the sacred name of God—Amen." We have already observed the part he bore in the wording of the Thirty-second Article of the Constitution. That Article forbade any person who denied the "being of God," or the "Divine authority of either the Old or New Testament," to hold office in North Carolina. Yet from the day the Constitution was signed almost to the day of his death, Harnett held office under that Constitution and frequently took the oath to support it. Harnett was a Mason, and held a position of no less dignity than Deputy Grand Master of North America, having jurisdiction over the entire continent. As Mr. Haywood says, "it is needless to tell a Mason" that Harnett was not an atheist.   'From time immemorial," he continues, "it has been held that no unbeliever is a fit person to be initiated into the mysteries of the Order. It was so in the Dark Ages; in 1722 it was reiterated in the *Charges of a Freemason*, and it is still a law of the Order. Whether a

[1] State Rec., XXII, 886.

slave to no sect, a slave to all sects, a Christian,
Unitarian, Jew, or Mohammedan, would not be
called into question, provided Harnett believed
in God—Nature's God, the God of all things
in heaven above, in the earth beneath, and the
water under the earth—but, whatever may have
been his personal views in a doctrinal way on the
subject of religion, belief in God he surely professed when he became a Mason." [1] Finally,
no atheist could have borne the relation to the
Church that Harnett bore. He was a vestryman
of St. James' Parish, Wilmington, and as such
was probably a communicant. At any rate, he
was no atheist, and his refusal of the cup on his
deathbed must have arisen from some other
cause than infidelity.

The glimpses which Harnett's letters give
us into his domestic affairs reveal a happy home
life. His wife, Mary Grainger, daughter of
Joshua Grainger, Jr., was a member of a large
family, long and prominently connected with
the history of the Cape Fear. [2] They had no
issue. Harnett's residence at Maynard, afterwards called Hilton, just outside the town of
Wilmington, was standing until within recent
years. The house, surrounded by a grove of
splendid oaks and luxuriant cedars, stood at
the end of a "magnificent avenue of live oaks,"
on an eminence of the east bank of the Cape

---

[1] The Beginnings of Freemasonry in North Carolina and Tennessee,
51—58.

[2] MS. notes of A. M. Waddell and W. B. McKoy.

Fear just above Wilmington, and commanded a fine view of the river. It was a brick structure described as being "of a type frequently used in colonial times, distinguished by the gambrel roof. Its interior woodwork was of red cedar, and of elaborate and ornate finish. The window and door frames were very broad, also of cedar. * * * Including the basement it contained twelve rooms."[1]   Griffith J. McRee, writing in 1846, says:[2] "The house was built by Cornelius Harnett; in front is a stone with his name and date of the erection. * * * If such houses as Hilton and Hyrneham were built at a very early period the fact proves a degree of taste, refinement and opulence on the part of the builders which has not been equaled since their day. For these with one or two others of a similar style are still much the best mansions on the river out of the town."

A portrait of Harnett as he appeared in his home has been drawn for us by the pen of Archibald Maclaine Hooper. Hooper's grandfather, Archibald Maclaine, and his father, George Hooper, brother of William Hooper, were among Harnett's intimate friends and his observations may be regarded as presenting the views of those eminent men as well as his own. Harnett's stature, he says, "was about five feet nine. In

---

1 Andrew J. Howell in the Charlotte Observer.
2 Unpublished letter to Gov. Swain, May 11, 1846, in the collections of the North Carolina Historical Society at the University of N. C. Copy in the collections of the North Carolina Historical Commission.

his person he was rather slender than stout.
His hair was of a light brown, and his e ˉes hazel.
The contour of his face was not striking; nor
were his features, which were small, remarkable
for symmetry; but his countenance was pleasing,
and his figure, though not commanding, was
neither inelegant nor ungraceful. * * * He
practiced all the duties of a kind and charitable
and elegant hospitality. * * * Easy in manner, affable, courteous, with a fine taste for
letters and a genius for music, he was always an
interesting, sometimes a fascinating companion.
He had read extensively for one engaged so much
in the bustle of the world, and he read with a
critical eye and inquisitive mind. * * * In
conversation he was never voluble. The tongue,
an unruly member in most men, was in him
nicely regulated by a sound and discriminating
judgment. He paid, nevertheless, his full quota
into the common stock, for what was wanting
in continuity or fullness of expression, was
supplied by a glance of his eye, the movement of
his hand, and the impressiveness of his pause.
Occasionally, too, he would impart animation
to his discourse by a characteristic smile of such
peculiar sweetness and benignity, as enlivened
every mind and cheered every bosom, within
the sphere of its radiance. He could be wary
and circumspect, or decided and daring, as
exigency dictated or emergency required. At

one moment abandoned to the gratification of sense, in the next he could recover his self-possession and resume his dignity. Addicted to pleasure, he was always ready to devote himself to business, and always prompt in execution. An inflexible republican, he - was beloved and honored by the adherents of monarchy amid the fury of a civil war."

Of Cornelius Harnett's public career but a word more need be said. Clearly he must be ranked as among American statesmen. Throughout his career his spirit was continental, his outlook national. Herein, indeed, lies the real significance of his services. Approaching his career from this point of view, we shall no longer think of the revolutionary history of North Carolina as "an isolated fragment but an organic part of a larger whole"; while his contributions to that history will appear equally contributions to American history. For surely the revolutionary movement in North Carolina was as much a part of the continental movement toward urion and nationality as the movements in Massachusetts and Virginia; and, therefore, the work of Cornelius Harnett in directing that movement was as national in its significance as was the same work of Samuel Adams in Massachusetts, or of Patrick Henry in Virginia. Cornelius Harnett's work was always constructive. He never pulled down but that he might build

up. With a profound faith in popular government, he had in his nature none of the elements
of the demagogue. He appealed neither to the
passions nor to the prejudices of mankind. His
work lay not on the hustings, nor, though a
debater of ability, in the legislative hall, but
rather in the council chamber. His chief service
was executive in its nature. This work was the
backbone of the Revolution without which the
eloquence of the orator, the wisdom of the legis-
lator, and the daring of the soldier would have
been barren of results. Yet it was a work that
offered but little opportunity for display, and
brought but little fame. Its only opportunity
was for service, its only reward, a broken body
and a martyr's grave. Lacking the fiery eloquence of Ashe, the learning of Johnston, the
versatility of Caswell, without the halo which
surrounds the brows of Hooper, Hewes and
Penn, as the signers of the Declaration of Independence, Cornelius Harnett was inferior to
none of them in the services rendered to the
cause of independence, in his devotion to liberty,
his faith in mankind, and his love of country,
in whose cause "he fearlessly dared the dungeon
and the scaffold."

INDEX

Adams, John, 149–50.
Adams, Samuel, 79–80, 146.
Alexander, Hezekiah, 154.
Anson county committee of safety, 126.
Appropriation bills, 27.
Arms and ammunition, 94–95, 97, 162–163.
Articles of Confederation, 186–89.
Ashe, John, 22, 31, 32, 43, 45, 75, 81, 95, 98, 100, 101, 103.
Ashe, Samuel, 22, 56, 111, 154.
Assembly, quorum of, 28.
Attachment clause, See (Foreign Attachments.)
Avery, Waightstill, 111.

Bath committee of safety 93.
"Blackbeard," 10.
Bloodworth, Timothy, 22.
Bonnet, Stede, 10–11.
Boundary line, North and South Carolina, 70.
Boyd, Adam, 22.
Brunswick, 14, 16–17, 101.
Burke, Thomas, 142, 152, 179, 186, 188, 189, 192.
Burrington, Gov. George, 7, 12.

Campbell, Farquard, 56.
Cape Fear, 9; inhabitants of, 13, 20.
Cape Fear Section, 7–13.
Cape Fear Gazette, the, 31.
Caswell, Richard, 81, 82, 117, 173, 177, 178.
Clinton, Sir Henry, 116, 118, 155, 162.
Collet, Capt. John, 98, 99.
Committees of safety, 79–80, 86, 107.
"Common Sense," 139.
Coor, James, 111, 154.
"Conservatives," 152.
Constitution, the North Carolina, 152, 172–78.
Continental Association, 84, 85, 91.
Continental Congress, 81, 181.
Continental troops, 105, 155.
Convention of 1769, 53–54.
Cornell, Samuel, 64.
Cornwallis, Lord, 116, 118.
Council of Safety, 153–54, 160–61.
Council of State, 178.
Court-law, the, 70–78.
Craige, Maj. James H., 195.
Cray, William, 178.
Cruizer, the, 100.

Dartmouth, Lord, 100.
Declaration of Independence, 169–172.
Declaratory Act, 48, 69.
DeRosset, Moses John, 22.
Diligence, the, 32.
District committees of safety, 108.
Dobbs, the, 33, 36.
Dobbs, Gov. Arthur, 26.
Dunmore, Lord, 114, 115.
Dry, William, 34, 35, 79, 178.

Eaton, Thomas, 111, 154, 178.
Edenton committee of safety, 93
Edwards, Isaac, 75.

Foreign attachments, 70–78.
Fort Johnston, 98, 99, 101.
French and Indian War, 25.

General Washington, the, 163.
Gerry, Elbridge, 148–49.
Glasgow, James, 178.
Grainger, Mary, wife of Cornelius Harnett, 201.
Granville county committee of safety, 126.
Harnett, Cornelius, Senior, 17–19.
Harnett, Cornelius, Age, 193, 194. Alderman of Wilmington, 23. Assembly, career in, 23, 24, 26, 42; on committees of, 25, 27–28, 29, 43, 59, 75, 76, 80; thanked by, 191–92. Battle of Lexington, 93; of Moore's Creek Bridge, 118. Birth, 20. Captured by British, 196. Committee of correspondence, 80. Committees of safety, chairman of, 87–88, 91; master-spirit of, 87–89. Conference with Quincy, 78–80. Constitution of North Carolina, contributions to, 174–78. Continental Association, enforces the, 48, 55, 56. Continental Congress, elected to, 180, 192; sets out for, 180; takes seat in, 181; discomforts of situation, 181, 189; letters written from, 182; policies advocated, 183; advocates larger army, 183; taxation, 183–84; opposes depreciated paper currency, 185; denounces greed of merchants, 185; on for-